Teri—
Thanks for being the best sister-in anyone could ask for! forget the underfur!

Southeast of Heaven

A Metalhead's Journey

By Don de Leaumont

Love ya Tons!

Don

Southeast of Heaven:
A Metalhead's Journey

Cover art by Tommy Smith.
Edited by Katherine Turman
Proofread by Victoria Basnuevo

Printed by Amazon Direct Publishing

First printing edition 2020.
ISBN Paperback: 978-1677759699

For more information:
www.thegreatsouthernbrainfart.com
www.facebook.com/thegreatsouthernbrainfart

This book is dedicated to the man who is responsible for me being the open, free-thinking, free-speaking asshole that I am today. Even though we struggled to communicate, music seemed to be the thing that brought us together. I miss you, Dad, and yes, I still have my debut W.A.S.P album, and I love it whether you like it or not.
I know you'd be judgemental, snarky, and proud.

Me & my folks.
Metairie, LA, 1975

Welcome to My...
Whatever This Is

Writing about yourself is kind of fucked-up, isn't it? It implies that there are people who would give a RATT's (yes, like the band) ass about your life story. So, why am I here then? My life isn't more extraordinary than anyone else's, but I've had some amazing experiences, and I hope some of you may relate to them.

What you are about to read is a collection of stories from my introduction to Heavy Metal music in the 1980s to my current life as a hard rock/metal blogger. It's the story of how a fat kid who was hated by girls and picked on and bullied relentlessly ended up becoming an independent writer hanging out and interviewing some of his heroes including RATT, Cinderella, Megadeth, Alice Cooper, and Bruce Dickinson of Iron Maiden.

Even if you're not a fan of Heavy Metal (like my wife) or only know Ozzy from his reality TV shows (like my in-laws), I hope that you'll be entertained by these stories and maybe see Heavy Metal music a little differently (it's not just noise!!). And for those of you that have spent countless hours listening to records that were targeted by Tipper Gore and the Parents Music Resource Center, Friday nights reading interviews in *RIP Magazine,* and more nights than you can remember being pressed up against the barricade at a sweaty and rowdy show, I hope you find a bit of yourself in these stories. Maybe they will inspire you to pull out your old albums and reconnect with a band or song. Or to get online and find yourself a new favorite band.

I have tried to be as honest and accurate as possible, but hey, I'm a storyteller from New Orleans after all, so there may be an embellishment here and there. Just where? I'll never tell. And yes, I had this book edited and proofread, but brace yourself, there's still some shitty grammar and typos (sorry Victoria), and more fucks and shits than you can count (sorry Mom).

As Ozzy said so prophetically in his song "Crazy Train," ALL ABOARD!

Me & my dad with my first skateboard.
Metairie, LA, 1986

Me & my dad sharing smug smiles.
Atlanta, GA, 2012

Love Me? Hate Me?
Well, Thank My Dad

My dad and I didn't have the best of relationships. My father viewed success and happiness by how much money someone made whereas I viewed success and happiness as doing what you truly love to do regardless of how rich you are. While we may not have had a lot in common or even talked all that much, one of the things we did share was a love and a passion for music.

I can remember my dad and I sitting in the living room as he played Styx's *The Grand Illusion*. "Donald, do you hear that? Now THAT is good music. Listen to his voice and listen to the arrangement of this song. This is what good music is all about." He'd put on albums by Joan Baez, Crosby Stills and Nash, or Buffy Sainte Marie then switch gears with Iron Butterfly's *In a Gadda DaVida*. My dad loved great vocalists and well-crafted songs.

My dad's taste in music was as broad and diverse as mine is today. I can still remember him telling me, "Donald, I don't care if it's polka music or if it's Heavy Metal music. If you like it and speaks to you, then it's good music. You need to be able to stand by your opinions and argue your case for why it's good." He always told me never to let the general public dictate to me what I should like. Just because it's on the radio and everyone likes it doesn't make it good.

Back in the '80s, when most parents were forbidding their kids to listen to the "evil" Ozzy Osbourne, my dad was listening to the *Tribute* album. He dug it. He thought Ozzy was cool and that "Goodbye to Romance" was "… way better than that Black Sabbath shit."

"But dad, Sabbath is awesome."

"No," he said, "Sabbath was loud, and Ozzy couldn't sing his way out of a wet paper bag, but this song is really good though. That guitar player is just amazing."

In our dysfunctional relationship, music seemed to be the thing that would bring us together. It was something we could talk about, something we could bond over without ever having serious "heart-to-heart" talks or "sit-downs." A lot of times, it would just be us sitting there, quietly listening to an album and him asking me what I liked about it and then him telling me what he thought about it.

Much like mine, dad's opinions were brutal and he stood by them. Dad thought Poison was shitty; he considered Tesla and Cinderella to be the cream of the crop; he was impressed to find that Iron Maiden was innovative and intelligent. Dad felt the same way about Metallica after listening to *Master of Puppets* with me. "I can tell by looking at their song titles that these guys have something to say," he said, looking at the back of my *Master of Puppets* album. "I'm glad I can read the lyrics here because I can't understand a goddamn thing that guy's saying, but I get it. He's angry, and it comes through. This is a very folk music form of expression but with way more volume." Mind = Blown.

In addition to encouraging me to have my own opinions and to stand by them, he taught me to respect the opinions of others. And to know that the people whose opinions I was trying to respect, may not respect me. When I started doing my music blog, The Great Southern Brainfart, in 2009, my dad loved hearing my stories about interviewing bands, going to concerts, and hanging out backstage. He liked that I was making friends with bands, but that I was also pissing some bands off with bad reviews. He said, "Donald, you're doing what you always wanted to do, and you're good at it. I'm glad you're speaking your mind, but be careful. You might get punched in the face over some of this shit."

Over the next thirty years, music was the thread that bound us together. My father passed away on August 1st (Jerry Garcia's birthday) of 2012. To this day, whenever I hear a new album or band, I can't help but wonder what my dad would have thought of it. I think he would've loved Jess and the Ancient Ones because they would have reminded him of Jefferson Airplane. I suspect he would have thought Old James was a badass rock and roll band and that he would have liked Jorn Lande because he's such a powerful metal vocalist. Love me or hate me, you can thank (or damn) my father for inspiring me to be the man I am today. So, if you've ever wondered where I get my snarky, opinionated nature, now you know.

Me, Jimmy, & my kid brother Dwayne on my birthday.
Metairie, LA, 1980-something

In the Beginning

Back in 1983, shit was very different. Postage was $0.20, bread was $0.66, and you could get a fucking Big Mac for $0.95. I was just another fat-ass kid with a bowl cut attending a Catholic school in New Orleans, Louisiana. Kids hated me. I never really quite figured out why, but it's always the fat kid who gets the shit end of the stick. I tried to fit in. I tried to convince kids that I liked Prince and thought Duran Duran was awesome, but I wasn't a good liar. I thought Culture Club had a few catchy songs and ZZ Top was kind of cool, but it wasn't enough. I was that odd, fucked-up puzzle piece unable to fit in with the rest of them. After a while, I gave up trying and just said, "Fuck it," and I went on about my day.

Although I had two parents at home, a kid brother, and a room of my own, my life lacked any passion. I didn't have anything I could call my own. At school, I saw all these kids having fun with each other while I hid in the back of the schoolyard praying to God they wouldn't come over and beat the shit out of me for sheer enjoyment. This happened quite a bit, and like anything else, after a while, you get used to it. "Oh look, it's a Wednesday, time to get myself pushed to the ground and be forced to kiss some asshole's shoe." Yeah, sounds like fun, huh? Stick with me…my life gets better, I promise!

But it's shit like this that can damn near break a kid. Even back then, it wasn't unheard of to read about some kid offing themselves because they couldn't take the unending crap that was being dealt to them daily. Not me though. Something in me wanted to fight physically, mentally, and emotionally. I just knew there was something more out there, something I could identify with and call my own. Unfortunately, I didn't know what it was, so I endured the schoolyard.

A year later, in 1984, I saw a video on *Friday Night Videos* (we didn't have cable yet so no MTV for me) for a song called "We're Not Gonna Take It" by Twisted Sister. I had never seen anything like it before. They were insane-looking, loud, obnoxious… and I fucking loved every second of it. That song and the video spoke to me. I couldn't believe my eyes or my ears. A bunch of old dudes who spoke for and to this ten-year-old kid. I felt like they were singing my life story back to me. I immediately ran out to Warehouse Records and Tapes and bought the cassette for *Stay Hungry*. I didn't know it then, but that moment marked the start of my journey.

My mother was a hard-working lady. She worked at a daycare center in Metairie, Louisiana called Athania Parkway. Don't bother looking for it; it's not there anymore. Anyway, they had an after-school program for older kids, and I would end up there every day after school. One day, I was sitting at a table, and across the room was this overweight kid who didn't look much different from me. He had headphones on and was playing drums on his plastic school box. I went over and asked him what he was listening to, and he says, "Twisted Sister." I told him how much I loved them and introduced myself to him. He told me his name was Jimmy.

Jimmy seemed like a cool dude and immediately asked me, "So who else do you listen to besides Twisted Sister?"

I was honest "Man, whatever's on the radio. I like Bryan Adams, and that band Toto is kind of cool."

Jimmy just laughed at me and said, "Man, you need to listen to some other bands." That day we became the best of friends. Beyond our love for Twisted Sister and their vocalist, Dee Snider, we had a lot in common. We went to different schools, but we were both the fat kid, outcasts who were looking for someone and something to latch on to.

It seemed like Jimmy had it all figured out, impressing me with the list of bands that he liked. "Have you ever heard Mötley Crüe? How about RATT? Scorpions? Iron Maiden?" I just shook my head, but I remember thinking, *If Jimmy likes these bands, they must be cool.* He invited me over to his house for a sleepover one weekend. I went over there and brought along my best Transformers. Jimmy had Optimus Prime, which was the shit at the time. Optimus Prime was the biggest of all the Transformers. We were hanging out in his room playing with our Transformers when I heard loud music coming from the room next door. "What is that?" I asked.

"That's my brother, Jay. Let's go see him." We knocked on his door, and there he was: long hair, muscle shirt, jeans, and loud music blasting out of his stereo. I felt how Beavis and Butthead felt whenever Todd came around. I was like, "Whoa. This dude is awesome."

His room was covered in crazy posters. Twisted Sister, Iron Maiden, Scorpions, Black Sabbath, and some guy who called himself Dio. I was intrigued by the intricacy of all the band logos. The artwork was kind of intense, but it didn't scare me. It made me feel like I was seeing a side of things that had been hidden from me. Jay put on some albums for us. He played us *Shout and the Devil* by Mötley Crüe and then *Love at First Sting* by Scorpions. Then he played an album that would change my life forever: Iron Maiden's *Number of the Beast*. I felt like a door to my soul had been opened. My heart raced, my blood seemed to pump faster, and I wanted more. Jay sent me home with some dubbed cassettes, planting the seed that would launch a thirty-year-journey into the world of Heavy Metal.

Oh no he's got my album in his hand.
Me & the lead singer of Zebra, Randy Jackson.
Atlanta, GA, 2018

Me, my brother Dwayne, & Lilian Axe.
Atlanta, GA, 1994

New Orleans Metal, Brah...

Metalheads are always trying to find each other. In a Catholic school where all the guys have bowl cuts and wear uniforms, you were either asked or found yourself asking, "Hey, brah. You into metal?" and hoping the answer would be, "Yeah, I'm into metal." Then it was on to "Who are you into?" My list was typical—Iron Maiden, Judas Priest, Dio, Twisted Sister, RATT, Krokus (yes, I said Krokus), but then sometime around '85 or '86 I was asked, "Do you like Zebra?" The only thing I knew about them was that they had a great song called "Who's Behind the Door" on their *Masters of Metal* album. Then someone gave me a copy of their debut album, and I was floored.

Zebra quickly became one of my favorite bands, and at the time, they were the biggest band in New Orleans even though they lived in New York (but that's another story). Pretty soon, everyone I knew had a copy of that album. It was a running joke that if you were born in New Orleans in 1984, you got a copy of the first Zebra album with your birth certificate. Of course, this just made me want to know if there were any other bands in New Orleans making music I might love. Low and behold, I was about to open up a portal into a whole world.

Eventually, I was tipped off to the fact that there were some incredible Heavy Metal bands out there playing the music I loved and kicking ass right in my hometown. Up to this point, the only other New Orleans band I knew about was the Neville Brothers, so to find that there were other bands out there doing hard rock and metal was super exciting.

The bad news was that these bands mostly played bars down in the French Quarter or in and around New Orleans, and I wasn't even close to being old enough to go. The good news was that I lived just outside of New Orleans in Metairie, where there were like a zillion Catholic schools, and one of them, St. Christopher, had a gymnasium that was run by the CYO (that's the Catholic Youth Organization). The CYO would rent the gym out to bands that would play all-ages shows, and some of them were Heavy Metal bands. This was some exciting shit because I could finally see some of the bands that I had heard about.

I saw more bands than I can remember, but some made huge impressions on me, whether I liked them or not. On the heavier spectrum, bands like Soilent Green, Acid Bath, and Graveyard Rodeo were doing their thing but they were just a bit too much for me. I was more into the melodic bands like Razor White, Victorian Blitz, Dark August, and Lillian Axe that reminded me of music I already loved, like Iron Maiden and Mötley Crüe.

Victorian Blitz was fronted by the now-legendary sludge master, Kirk Windstein of Crowbar. I can still remember his mullet and them doing one the best covers of Iron Maiden's "Phantom of the Opera." Razor White was pretty much Skid Row before Skid Row appeared, and Lillian Axe was the band we all thought would go on to be huge. Even before they were signed, they were opening for bands in arenas. After they got signed to a record deal with MCA Records, RATT's Robbin Crosby produced their debut record. They even had a video on MTV. Unfortunately, it was "trashed" on MTV's "Smash or Trash" segment. I don't remember who the smash was, but unfortunately, it wasn't our beloved Lillian Axe.

I also dug some heavier thrash bands like Exhorder and Killer Elite. I never got to see Killer Elite live, but they had this amazing song called "The Ship Sailed On" that was on a local radio compilation album. I never heard anything else from them, but that one song made such an impact on me that I'm still talking about them nearly thirty years later.

Getting to see so many of these great New Orleans bands in my youth had a magical impact on me. I mean, it was one thing to see bands like Mötley Crüe and RATT and Iron Maiden on MTV, but to see bands playing a school gym and sounding every bit as good as those "major" bands was truly inspiring. These bands were playing in my backyard, and they were fucking killing it. Even though they weren't huge, they had lights, massive drum kits, sometimes even stairs, and ramps. They made it seem attainable, like I could do it too...or at least try my damndest.

Many of these New Orleans artists went on to be successful and became legends in their own right. Bands like Crowbar, Lillian Axe, Corrosion of Conformity, and Eye Hate God all have members who once ruled the night at St. Christopher's CYO back in the '80s. So, regardless of whether I'm a fan of their current bands, I have the biggest respect for them sticking it out. I owe them all a debt of gratitude for reminding this fat little kid from Metairie that you didn't have to be from Hollywood or play arenas to be a star.

Still in my record collection & still gets played

K-Tel Hell

After getting a taste of metal music, I was like a soon-to-be junkie who just had his first hit of smack. As corny as it sounds, I was addicted to Heavy Metal. If they had long hair and were loud, I loved it. After some initial guidance from Jimmy and his older brother Jay, I was ready to dive deep into the world of Heavy Metal. The only problem was there were a lot of shitty bands out there (Autograph, I'm talking to you). There was no way in hell that I was going to be able to find all the great bands out there on my own. Eventually, I would discover music magazines like *Circus* and *Hit Parader*, but until then, K-Tel was the gateway to some of my greatest discoveries.

For those of you who are either too young to know or don't know, K-Tel was the master of mixtapes and LPs. K-Tel put out all kinds of crap. They put out shit like Disco Dance Party albums and

Songs to Make Out To. Most importantly, they put out the *Masters of Metal* compilations. I had seen them in the local K&B drugstores in New Orleans, and one day one grabbed my eye. *White Hot: Masters of Metal.* The album cover had a fucking fingerless gloved hand gripping a guitar neck that had something like 39 frets rising from what looked like the top of the sun into outer space. To a kid who had just discovered metal, this was bad to the fucking bone.

The best thing about these K-Tel albums was that they were cheap as hell. You could buy the album for about $7.99 and the cassette for $4.99 or something like that. I gazed over the tracklist, and what excited me the most was that I hadn't heard a lot of these songs. Yeah, I heard Twisted Sister and, of course, Zebra (New Orleans homeboys), but what about this band called Rush? What about Triumph? Who the fuck were these guys? I didn't know, but I couldn't wait to find out.

I put the album on my Realistic turntable, and the first song was "Rock You Like a Hurricane." It kicked ass, but I was already down with the Scorpions at this point. Slade was up next with "Run Runaway," and I remember thinking that this was some awful shit. But the rest of the album…well, there were two valuable things I learned from *White Hot!*:

1. Rush was one of the weirdest fucking bands I'd ever heard, but "Distant Early Warning" was so fucking cool. Looking back, I know now that listening to it slowly opened a door that I wouldn't find myself walking through for another five or so years (we'll get to that story later).

2. After hearing the song "Heaven and Hell" by Black Sabbath, I realized that a new frontman had replaced Ozzy. Up until

this point, I had no fucking clue Ronnie James Dio, the guy that I knew solely as Dio with songs like "Holy Diver" and "Rainbow in the Dark," sang for Black Sabbath. Mind = Blown.

Still in junkie mode, "Heaven and Hell" had me heading down to Warehouse Records and Tapes to buy my very first Black Sabbath album. I asked the stoner dude behind the counter what Sabbath album I should buy that had Dio on it, and he said, "Dude, do you have *Paranoid* yet?"

I said, "Is Dio on that one?"

"No," he answered.

"Well, I don't want it then."

He just laughed, walked over to the Sabbath bin, and handed me a copy of *Live Evil*. I asked if it was any good, and he said, "It's Dio singing in Sabbath. Of course, it's good." Nothing more had to be said. I took that album home, and there, my love for Black Sabbath began.

K-Tel was my entry to metal masters like Sabbath, Krokus, Triumph, and Dokken. It also served as a powerful reminder of what to stay the fuck away from. I mean, who needs to be listening to Slade (even if Quiet Riot did cover their songs) and Y&T? Sure as hell not me. Neither of these bands musically connected with me, and I thought Y&T came across as trying too hard while Slade sounded dated, bland, and unexciting. It was also on a K-Tel album that I heard Rainbow's "Street of Dreams" featuring lead vocalist Joe Lynn Turner. I thought this song was so corny and weak, and it is what kept me from diving into Rainbow for many years, only to discover later that Rainbow was fronted earlier in their career by, you guessed it, RONNIE JAMES DIO!

.

Me & Dio guitarist Craig Goldy, the
man who dared me to dream.
Atlanta, GA, 2019

Dare to Dream & Never Say Never

Ronnie James Dio was a Heavy Metal icon I couldn't avoid if I tried. After owning so many K-Tel *Masters of Metal* compilations, "Rainbow in the Dark" became an earworm that led me to the mystical world of Dio. At the time, Dio's newest release was *Sacred Heart*. While I thought it was a good album, it didn't resonate with me as a whole. That being said, songs like "King of Rock N' Roll," "Sacred Heart," and "Like the Beat of a Heart" were undeniably kick-ass tunes. But it was the song "Rock N' Roll Children" that struck a chord. This song told a story of lost children running away from society to escape its oppressive grasp so they could live in their own world. Now, *this* was something I could relate to.

I backtracked and picked up Dio's previous two albums, *Holy Diver* and *Last in Line*. These were the shit. I loved them and found myself lost in the fantasy stories that Dio created in the songs. When

I got older, these stories would take on a much more personal meaning.

Dio's 1987 *Dream Evil* was the album where I finally found myself connecting to the lyrical content of the songs on a deep level. The stories that he told in songs like "Night People," "Dream Evil," and "All The Fools Sailed Away" were not just stories. There were messages in there that I would find myself completely relating to. Lyrics such as "Don't go to the edge of rainbows. Don't close your eyes. Like things that can't be real. The truth lies." actually meant something to me. I think being a little older and more attuned to the deep lyrical content of Dio's music made me understand those earlier songs. Suddenly, songs like "Last In Line," "Rainbow in the Dark," and "Don't Talk to Strangers" took on a much deeper meaning.

My connection to *Dream Evil* grew stronger the more I listened to it, and the song "I Could've Been a Dreamer" was the one that spoke volumes to me. I can vividly remember the precise moment that it became *my* song and a huge part of my life. One evening my dad came into my room, cranky as fuck after a long day at work. "Quit playing your guitar, Donald," he said, "You should be doing your homework. Don't make me regret buying you that thing."

I replied, "Dad, but I'm practicing so I can be a rockstar someday."

My dad shook his head and said, "That's an impossible life, son. You need to think realistically."

After this exchange, I put on my *Dream Evil* vinyl, and for some reason, looking down at the album's label, I put on my headphones and carefully placed the needle on the track "I Could've Been a Dreamer." The song filled my mind as I laid on my bed with my eyes closed. Here comes the chorus: *"I could've been a dreamer. I could've been a shooting star. I could've been a dreamer 'cause dreams are what we are."* I found myself crying because after being shot down by my father, here was this guy, who was older than my dad encouraging me to be a dreamer.

This was some truly heavy shit. It made me wonder if my dad was ever a dreamer. Was he shot down by his dad, told to conform to what society expected him to be as a grown man? Before his death, my father told me that he was envious of me because I dreamed big and never compromised. That meant a lot to me, and in a lot of ways, I have Dio to thank for that. Dio told me always to be a dreamer and to be a shooting star.

I had an encounter with Ronnie after a Black Sabbath show in 1992. Ronnie was holding court on the side of the stage. He was talking, taking pictures, and signing stuff. He looked me dead in the eye and smiled. For those who know me, I am rarely, if ever, speechless, but I couldn't find the words to say what an inspiration and positive influence he was on me. He reached over, pulled a setlist off of a road case, handed it to me, and smiled. I just walked away. That was the magic of Ronnie James Dio. He knew his fans so well that he could look into our eyes and know what we wanted to say when we couldn't.

Dio's words, music, and life meant the world to me, and when we lost him to cancer in 2010, a huge part of me felt lost as well. I not only lost one of my favorite musicians but a man who guided me through some of the hardest times of my youth. I kept Ronnie close in my heart as always, knowing that while his music would live forever, I would never see him again. Or would I?

Sometime around 2017, it was announced that a tour would be launched called *Dio Returns*, which would feature a Dio hologram in addition to the members of Dio Disciples (former members of Dio) and guest vocalists. Just the mention of this Dio hologram tour had me wanting to beat myself to death with my own shoes. "This is a travesty!" I would say. "They're tarnishing the legacy of Dio! His bandmates should know better. Why are they even behind this?" I would ask.

There were so many emotions tied to this whole concept. I was angry, I was intrigued, I was angry that I was intrigued, I was defensive, I was hurt. I wrote an article about my disapproval of the whole idea and got into debates on Facebook over it. Eventually Craig Goldy, longtime guitarist and best friend of Ronnie's, tried to argue his case with me online, resulting in a pretty nasty back and forth argument. At some point, Craig sent me a private message that said, "Don, I'm tired of all this typing. Please call me at…" Shit. *Is Craig going to tear me a new asshole? Will he ream me for being a dick?* I wasn't sure, but I was sure of one thing; I wasn't going to turn the opportunity to talk to Dio's former right-hand man. I called Craig and was prepared to stand my ground and defend my opinion.

I braced myself for the war of words to continue, but instead, I was greeted with a kind, warm voice that said, "Don, I'm glad you called. It's easier to talk than to type." For the next two hours, Craig would ask about me, what Ronnie meant to me as a young dude, and what his legacy meant to me now. Craig, in turn, would share amazing stories about his time with Ronnie, the things he would say, and the things he would do for his fans. It was a very moving and emotional conversation that eventually brought us both to tears and, much like Ronnie, would've loved to see, brought us together as friends.

But, at the end of the call, I told Craig that I still didn't agree with the hologram tour idea. He told me, "Don, if this tour ever makes it to Atlanta, please come out and be my guest. I want you to see it before you pass judgment. If you see it and you feel something, please share it, if you don't like it, share that too, but at least come to your conclusion after seeing it for yourself." That, to me, was a very fair offer, so I agreed—I mean, come on, when Dio's best friend asks you be his guest at a show and says it's ok to write a snarky review about it, you don't say no!

During the European leg of the *Dio Returns* tour, I heard mixed messages, just as I thought I would. I did notice, however, that many of the "hate" comments were from people who didn't attend the shows. Those who did attend the show had so many great things to say. They called it "emotional," "moving," and "an unforgettable experience." But I called it bullshit. How could a hologram move anyone?

Sometime in late March 2019, it was announced that the *Dio Returns* tour would be hitting North American shores. Once it was official and the dates were released, there was a June 3rd date set for Atlanta at Center Stage Theater. Craig messaged and assured me that he still wanted me there, and I took him up on it. I reminded him that I would be honest, regardless of our friendship. He accepted that, and I forged forward, waiting for the date to arrive.

The *Dio Returns* tour would feature longtime bandmates and friends of Ronnie's, including my new pal Craig Goldy on guitar, Simon Wright on drums, Scott Warren on keys, and Dio Disciples bassist Bjorn Englen. The tour would also feature two guest singers who were two of my favorites; Oni Logan (Lynch Mob/Dio Disciples) and Tim "Ripper" Owens (Judas Priest/Iced Earth). It was also reported that the stage production would be of epic proportions, just like Ronnie would have wanted.

I'm not going to lie to you, the closer the tour got to Atlanta, the more excited I got. I was going to meet Craig Goldy, my all-time favorite Dio guitarist. But I was also nervous—I mean, there was a good chance I was going to have to write that I hated the show. If you read my blog, you know that even a friendship with Craig Goldy can't keep me from spewing my brainfart honesty.

I purposely didn't tell more than a few close friends that I was going. I didn't want to hear negative thoughts—I mean, more negative than my own already were. I wanted to hold to my side of the bargain with Craig and attend the show unbiased, my guard let down, and my mind completely opened.

Entering the venue, I did something I rarely do these days; I headed straight for the barricade and staked out my spot. Luckily, I had just missed Love/Hate which was a good thing because I leaned more towards the Hate side of them. I believe Center Stage Theater holds somewhere near 1000 people, but there were only about 300 people there. They had the sides of the theater curtained off, which made sense because unless you are looking head-on or slightly to the side, you wouldn't be able to see the hologram.

As I waited for the show to start, to my right were two young guys who looked like they were probably fresh out of high school. I struck up a conversation with one of them and asked how he was feeling about the show. "Dio is one of my all-time favorites. I wasn't old enough to see him when he was alive, so this is my chance to see it done in a pretty cool way." When I asked if he was bothered that it was a hologram, he laughed and said, "If I were, I wouldn't be here." Fair enough, wee lad!

The stage was a set of Stonehenge-shaped LED screens. Think the big Stonehenge as opposed to the small one from *Spinal Tap*. All of a sudden, the house lights went down, and the LED screens lit up with visuals. The intro to "Sacred Heart" that was projected on a screen on his 1985 *Sacred Heart* tour appeared on the screen, and the place went nuts. "Welcome, my children." The band took their positions on stage and kicked things off with "King of Rock and Roll." The visuals were nothing less than astonishing, and then suddenly, Dio "himself" manifested from a ball of fire and started singing.

Once again, the crowd went wild. I stood there dumbfounded, and next thing I knew, I was throwing horns and singing along. It was crazy seeing him again but in the form of a hologram. While I will admit that the visual and technology aspect of the hologram was cool, I didn't feel any emotion. I was entertained, but no emotions would come until the performances of Ripper Owens and Oni Logan.

For the second song, Ripper took the stage to huge applause and announced that this was a celebration of the life and the music of Ronnie James Dio. With that, he said, "If you listen to fools..." and the crowd responded loudly with "the Mob Rules!" Then the band kicked right into the song. Ripper, as many political differences as I've had with this guy, is a goddamn metal god in his own right. He delivered that song as his life depended upon it, and suddenly, the emotions welled. The energy, the fire, the passion, it was all there, and it resonated with the audience.

Oni Logan then took the stage and said, "This song needs no introduction." The opening notes of "Children of the Sea" rang out, and once again, the audience roared excitedly. I couldn't take my eyes off of Logan; he's not a showboating kind of vocalist or someone just going through the motions. Logan's passion and dedication to the song were loud and clear and cut me to the bone. It choked me up and took me back to the time when I would listen to this song and feel like Dio understood me even when I felt nobody else did. I started crying. It was powerful; I remember being one of those lost children.

Seeing Goldy play live for the first time in all my years as a Dio fan proved to me why he's my favorite Dio guitarist. He knows how to capture the vibe of all of the songs. The quietest of the quiet and the heaviest of heavy, he exercises his dynamic playing with a lot of feel and soul.

As the show drew to a close, we saw more of the Dio hologram singing, but this time, what made it cool was that he was joined on stage by Ripper and Logan. They closed out with a mind-blowing rendition of "We Rock" that featured hologram Ronnie, Logan, and Ripper trading off verses. It was the first time I felt that the hologram had some captivating presence.

People, I would be a liar if I didn't say that *Dio Returns* was nothing short of spectacular. The musicianship was amazing, the vibe was outstandingly positive and fun, and the whole visual spectacle made for an unforgettable evening. I didn't find the Dio hologram to be a travesty or disrespectful. If anything, I honestly found it the least moving aspect of the show. I don't know if it's because I was lucky enough to see Dio in flesh and blood or if it's more that I viewed it as part of an astounding production.

It's been said by Wendy Dio, Ronnie's widow, and members of his band that *Dio Returns* is a celebration of the music of Ronnie James Dio, and they were not lying. In my opinion, it was probably the best way to pay tribute to this man who meant so much to me and millions of others. After seeing this show, I couldn't help but think that Ronnie would've thought that it was nothing but an honor to be remembered and to be able to come back from the dead to entertain fans both old and young, many timers and first-timers alike.

Dio Returns was a production with a lot of love, heart, blood, sweat, and tears. I walked in a doubter, and I left with my heart filled with happiness; but it wasn't because of a Dio hologram. It was because of the passion and the love put into the songs by his band and by the amazing Oni Logan and Ripper Owens. I would love to see Dio Disciples hit the road on their own more extensively, and even without the grandiose production, I know damn good and well that I would walk out of there experiencing the emotions that I felt that night. Yes, Dio has "returned," but let's not forget that along with him comes a cast of characters who proved to be the real stars of the show.

As I exited the venue, there was nothing but smiles on everyone's faces. I didn't hear anyone saying that it sucked or that it was a shit show like I thought it would be nearly two years previously. Hologram aside, Dio's Disciples brought the spirit of Ronnie James Dio back to the stage only to prove that you can't kill rock and roll, and you can't kill Dio.

For as long as there will be generations of Dio's Disciples, the message and legacy of Dio's music will live forever. With or without the hologram, I support these guys and thank them all for making me feel things I thought I'd never feel again. Long live rock and roll, long live Dio, and long live his songs. May they be the comfort for many young generations to come.

After the performance, I was escorted backstage, where I would finally come face to face with the friend who I once agreed to disagree with, Craig Goldy. It was an emotional meeting. He grabbed me and hugged me tight, looked at me, smiled, and said, "My friend, the dreamer."

We spoke about many things, but, of course, the thing we talked about most was Ronnie. He shared stories about what a kind, generous soul Ronnie was. He even told me a story about once, on tour, there was a group of fans waiting out in the snow to meet Dio. Ronnie invited the fans into the venue, took them to catering, fed them, and talked to every one of them while signing things and taking photos down to the last person. "That's the kind of person Ronnie was," Craig said. "Ronnie didn't have fans. He considered them his children."

Like all great things, the meeting between Craig and I had to come to an end. We said our good-byes outside the tour bus, exchanged hugs, and he once again thanked me for being me. "You have a true gift as a writer and a dreamer, and I'm so honored to be a part of your life and to have you as a brother. I love you." I broke down crying, and he just laughed, hugged me again, and said, "We are such criers, aren't we?"

Before leaving, I had Craig sign my *Intermission* EP, and on it, he wrote, "To my dear brother Don, dare to dream." I have not conformed to what society thinks a 45-year-old should be. I am living my dreams, and I continue to work hard and dream big. Without any compromise, I'm a dreamer, I'm a shooting star, and a dream is what I am. I dare to dream, and I do it every day.

Me, Scott, & Mike, just some miserable
devil-worshipping metalheads hanging out
in my poster covered bedroom.
Metairie, LA, 1980-something

The Satanic Panic

In the '80s, I was a full-blown metalhead. Studded bracelets and a denim jacket full of buttons with a Metallica *Ride the Lightning* back patch. I was wearing Judas Priest shirts, Iron Maiden shirts, Grim Reaper shirts, and I even had a Metallica shirt featuring a toilet with a hand coming out of it holding a knife and reading "Metal up Your Ass." Were my parents worried about me? Not at all. But I was forbidden to wear that Metallica shirt around my grandmother.

The '80s were an odd time for hard rock and metal music. Just like me, kids all over the world were listening to this incredible music that made us feel like we weren't alone and could rise above the shit going on in our lives. But at some point in the game, the music became an enemy of the state. Some of it was even deemed lethal and harmful. A few even believed that it might open the door to the souls of young children and allow Satan to enter them and cause them to do terrible things. And by terrible things, I mean smoke cigarettes, stay in their rooms reading magazines, and worst of all, have a good fucking time. An army of bored Washington homemakers led by Tipper Gore assembled to form the Parents Music Resource Committee (PMRC), and everyone from Madonna to W.A.S.P was on their shit list.

In a nutshell, the PMRC deemed certain music to be unsuitable for children, and the organization succeeded in having a law passed that any recorded materials that didn't meet their criteria of what was "good and wholesome" got a sticker slapped on the cover that read "Parental Advisory: Explicit Lyrics." Um…idiots. Didn't they know that would make us want to listen even more? I mean, I remember when I was a kid in a convenience store and on the top shelf would be the nudie mags. They always had the cover blacked out except for the cover girl's face and the magazine title. All I ever wanted was to see what the fuck was under that black bar. I mean, I wasn't stupid. I knew it was bare breasts but blocking it out made me want to see it that much more. Well, that's the effect that the Parental Advisory stickers had. When you tell a kid they can't have something, listen to something, or see something, chances are they will make sure they can by any means necessary.

At some point, the issue with Heavy Metal music shifted from being just obscene to being the music of the devil himself, fueling "The Satanic Panic." And no surprise, my Catholic school bought it. The nuns and teachers were urging parents to keep their kids away from all this sinful and rebellious music sweeping over the entire nation. I mean consider their evil names: Iron Maiden, Black Sabbath, Twisted Sister and W.A.S.P (which in case you don't know, stands for We Are Sexual Perverts). It was like metalheads were on the highway to hell, a path to eternal damnation. And if we owned *Shout at the Devil* by Mötley Crüe or *See You In Hell* by Grim Reaper, God was going to bitch slap us from the pearly gates straight to the bowels of hell.

It got worse when parents started blaming the music when kids committed suicide instead of taking responsibility for not paying attention to the mental and emotional state of their kids. In 1984, John Daniel McCollum's family sued Ozzy Osbourne because they believed that their son killed himself because of the song "Suicide Solution." Then there was the 1985 suicide pact of Raymond Belknap and James Vance that the families blamed on Judas Priest's song "Better By You, Better Than Me" from the *Stained Class* album. In October of 1988, journalist Geraldo Rivera compiled all of these stories, along with appearances from professed Satanic murderers, leaders of the Satanic Church and the Temple of Set, and supposed Satanism experts, for a television broadcast called "Satanism: Exposing Satan's Underground."

I vividly remember a note being sent home to our parents, urging them to watch this special with us. My mom and dad sat me down and said, "Geraldo Rivera is a nutcase, but we'll watch his dumb show." Luckily, my parents didn't buy it and said that while they were sad those kids killed themselves, it's likely that they addicted to drugs or that they were just "crazy" (mental health wasn't talked about in my family even though I come from a line of bipolar alcoholics). As for me, this was my first introduction to King Diamond, so if anything, I have Geraldo to thank for that.

After the show was over, we sat around, and the three of us had a cool conversation. My dad said, "Donald, I have no problem with you listening to any of this music. All I ask is that you bring it to me when you buy it, and let's talk about it together and see if there is anything you have questions about."

From that point on, my dad would check in with me about what I was listening to. He would ask me things like, "Does this music make you feel something? Does it make you want to do things? Does it make you mad? Happy?" Usually, my answer was "I like it because it's loud and fun to listen to. The artwork is awesome, and they have cool stages at their concerts." Well, that was good enough for him, so my continuing journey as a metalhead pretty much went uninterrupted until I bought the debut album from W.A.S.P. That's another story that we'll get to later.

The Satanic Panic and aftermath of Geraldo's show was pretty fucking crazy. Kids I knew were forbidden to listen to Heavy Metal music. They had to burn their shirts and get rid of all of their albums. It was insane. And it wasn't just the adults. The media brainwashing got to some of the kids. The one that shocked me the most was Jimmy, the kid who got me into metal. He burned all of his records in fear that he would be damned to hell if he continued to listen to them. He even stopped talking to me in case my evil was contagious.

Luckily, I still had one friend, Mike, who wasn't moved by any of it. Our folks continued to let us listen to metal music, and guess what? We didn't get into drugs (yet…I mean we were 12), we didn't drink booze (yet…again only 12), we didn't kill ourselves, and we didn't kill anyone else or any small animals. We maintained decent grades and managed to be good kids. We grew up to be somewhat respectable adults and contributed what we could to society in a positive way.

The Satanic Panic very well could have cost me my ability to freely listen to music had I not had parents who supported freedom of speech, but luckily, they knew it was nothing more than a scare tactic. And to be honest (and I'm sure this will piss Tipper Gore off), hard rock and metal music did far more good than bad in my personal life. It opened the door to conversations with my dad. It made me learn not to take everything so literally. It's just fucking music. Whether or not these guys were truly Satanists or not, their endgame was to entertain—and I was pretty fucking entertained. And because acts like Dio and Twisted Sister inspired a lost generation, I felt less alone and less misunderstood. Finally, it made me aware of the hypocrisy of organized religions, the general public, and the media. They were casting stones and conducting witch hunts while living in lavish homes, having affairs with porn stars, molesting children, and living up to their ears in crooked politics. If the Satanic Panic did anything for me, it made me love Heavy Metal music even more and made me more afraid of the ones who were fighting so hard to stop us from listening to it. I was—and still am— way less scared of King Diamond than I am of Geraldo Rivera.

I Wanna Rock! Me, my Twisted Sister shirt,
& my Jay Jay French sunglasses.
New Orleans, LA, 1984

Twisted Sister Saved My Life

How many times have you heard someone say, "Music saved my life?" I know it's cheesy, but for me, it did. If you've read this far, you know that in 1984, I was a fat, awkward kid plodding through the days at a Catholic school in New Orleans. I wanted nothing more than to be included and accepted, but I was made fun of, called names, and beaten up after school on a pretty regular basis. Sometimes, I even found myself wondering just how long I could put up with it.

I remember when I was 10, sitting on my bed listening to the *Stay Hungry* cassette and wondering how a band that didn't even know I exist could know me so well. I mean, it was like "We're Not Gonna Take It" and "I Wanna Rock" were speaking directly to me, telling me that it was going to be all right, that I wasn't alone and that there were probably millions of "me" out there. Twisted Sister was "my" band. They were a band who empowered misfits, and no matter what, we had to roll with the punches and never compromise who we were.

Just like the kid in the Twisted Sister videos, I started wearing a Twisted Sister button on my catholic school uniform. I would go to the record store, and I would buy every fucking Twisted Sister button I could because every time Sister Stickupherass would take my button away and send me to the office, I would show up the next day with a new one. It was my statement, it was me being me, and they weren't going to take that away from me.

Eventually, they "won" by suspending me. Sure, let the bullies who were kicking my ass daily get away with it, but send a kid home for wearing a goddamn Twisted Sister button. I waited in the office for my dad to come and pick me up with my head held low and feeling defeated. When we got home, my dad sat me down, and we had a heart-to-heart, him telling me that I had to stop wearing my Twisted Sister button because eventually, they would throw me out of school. Ok, so I would abide, but I didn't give up completely. I drew the "TS" logo on every notebook I had, and there wasn't a thing they could do about it. Don-1, Catholic School Assholes-0.

Once I had played the living hell out of *Stay Hungry*, off to Warehouse Records and Tapes I went to see what else I could find on my new heroes. It turns out they only had two other albums, but *Under the Blade* and *You Can't Stop Rock & Roll* were welcome additions to the arsenal. I didn't know it yet, but "I Am, I'm Me," "SMF," and "You Can't Stop Rock & Roll" were building up a confidence in me that was soon to be unleashed. These were my songs, and I felt as if they were written specifically for me. I even started wearing sunglasses purchased from Warehouse Records and Tapes, trying to emulate lead guitarist Jay Jay French.

At our school, when we went on field trips, we were allowed to wear "normal" clothes. That was when everyone would be wearing their trendy-ass Coca-Cola shirts, their Benetton shirts, and their Day-Glo jams, being, ya know, "cool." I told my dad that I wanted to wear my Twisted Sister shirt and jeans. Dad said, "You know that they're just going to pick on you more, right?" I told him I did, and dad said, "Well, then go out there, just be yourself, and stick to your guns, but be prepared for whatever comes your way."

On the day of the field trip, I sulked into school wearing my Twisted Sister t-shirt with Dee Snider's face taking up the whole front, my blue jeans, and cheap-ass K-Mart tennis shoes. The look on their faces was priceless. It's almost as if they didn't know what to do, but guess what? They just made even more fun of me. Following the field trip, the ass kickings got more frequent, but I was still not willing to back down.

One evening, I was at home nursing a black eye and listening to *Stay Hungry*. I must've listened to "We're Not Gonna Take It" on repeat about 15 times. In a rare moment, my father sat next to me and said, "You go to school tomorrow. When that bully comes up to you, regardless of how many people are standing behind him, you punch him in the face as hard as you can. You knock him out, and we'll figure it out together." I couldn't believe that he had said that. After our talk, I knew what I had to do. I couldn't take it anymore.

The next day, I arrived at school with yet another Twisted Sister button on my uniform and not giving a fuck. I was keeping to myself on the playground, reading a *Circus* magazine, when the kid who had been kicking my ass every day for two years straight approached me. He looked at me and said, "I can't believe you came to school today. You're dumber than I thought. Now lick my shoe." His friends were all behind him, laughing at me. I felt the years of torment building up in me like a shaken-up bottle of beer.

He took a step to push me, and with Twisted Sister as my guide (I could almost hear Dee Snider say, "DO IT, DON!"), I closed my eyes, made a fist, and swung my arm with everything I had. I know I connected with something, but I kept my eyes closed, waiting for the return punch... but it never came. I opened my eyes, ready to get the beating of my life, but instead, I saw him lying on the ground, his nose bleeding like a stuck pig. He was crying and yelling, "You hit me! You broke my nose!" His friends tore off running to tell the teachers. I was dragged off the school ground by a teacher then suspended for three days and told to write him a letter of apology. My father refused to make me write the letter and I took my three-day suspension with my head held high.

After all of that, guess what? I still wasn't cool. I wasn't popular or accepted, but I was left alone. I ate my lunch in peace, I hung out at recess and read my *Circus* magazines without being disturbed, and after school, I waited for my mom to pick me up out front instead of hiding behind the building only to run out when I saw her car. From that day on, I walked differently; I talked differently. I was a completely different kid. Twisted Sister pulled the strong, young man out of me who had been afraid to come out. I hate that I had to hit somebody to stand up for myself, but I don't regret it. And luckily, I've never been in another fight.

Every kid should have a Twisted Sister—whether it's Iron Maiden, Cannibal Corpse, Slipknot, or even fucking Lady Gaga. Everyone should have that connection with a band that makes them feel good and understand that they aren't out there alone. Twisted Sister was *my* band, my therapy, the friends that I didn't have. I've had the opportunity to meet a lot of my heroes in my life, but I've never met Twisted Sister. I hope that one day I can thank them in person for being there for me and tell them I will always be a Sick Motherfucking Friend of Twisted Sister. You can't stop Rock & Roll!

Me learning that heathen devil music.
Atlanta, GA, 1989

Me and my dad's favorite album.

Parental Guidance

My dad wasn't the "let's go play catch" type (not that I was an athletic kid), and we didn't have serious talks about politics or the news; but when we did talk, it was about music. And my dad had some opinions! He thought Ozzy Osbourne's guitarist Randy Rhoads was by far the best guitar player, while Eddie Van Halen was overrated. Even though he thought some stuff was pretty bad (Poison was "absolute hogwash"), he pretty much let me listen to what I wanted. That changed early in 1985.

One day, while perusing the aisle of the metal section at Warehouse Records and Tapes, an album by a band called W.A.S.P caught my eye. The cover image freaked me out, but it was so intriguing that I couldn't stay away from it. Not only did the guys look wicked as all fuck, but there was something about the way they were looking at *me* from this cover that was saying, "Bring us home, kid." I knew I needed this album, but the question remained, "What would my dad make of this?" I mean, the lead singer had a saw blade over his cock, and one of the songs was "L.O.V.E Machine."

I got home, and my dad said, "W.A.S.P., huh? Let's give this one a listen." As we sat down, my dad picked up the cover and looked at it. He flipped the record over and read the quote on the back out loud: "'The Gods You Worship are Steel. At the Altar of Rock N' Roll You Kneel.' Wow, that sounds really stupid." "I Wanna Be Somebody" kicked off the album, and I was digging it and started nodding my head. About halfway through the album, I asked, "Pretty good, huh?" He just looked at me and said, "Son, I don't care what you listen to, but you aren't using my money to buy a W.A.S.P album."

My dad didn't seem to mind the album cover or the song titles; he just thought W.A.S.P flat-out sucked. "We're taking this crap back and swapping it out for something better." He hauled me back to the record store and told the kid behind the counter, "My son bought this album, and these guys are crap. Can we swap it for something else?"

The kid just laughed and said, "Yeah, man, these guys do suck."

My dad took a break to listen to what was being played in the store and asked, "What's this you're playing?"

The kid answered, "This is Led Zeppelin *IV*, man."

My dad goes, "Now THIS is cool. Give him that one." So, I guess in a way, I can thank my dad for getting me my first Zeppelin album.

The way my dad reacted to the W.A.S.P album, I could only imagine what he was going to say when I got Ozzy Osbourne's *Bark at the Moon*. My friends' parents were like, "Ozzy is Satan. NO!" whereas my dad was like, "Let's listen to it." My dad decided the guitar playing was great and that he sang "way better than he did on that Black Sabbath crap." My dad ended up buying me both *Blizzard of Ozz* and *Diary of a Madman*. The three things I remember the most about listening to these albums with my dad was that 1) he thought "Goodbye To Romance" was a beautiful song, 2) he said "Diary of a Madman" had some of the best guitar playing he'd heard from any of the bands I listened to, and 3) that he used it as an opportunity to get one more dig in: "…and he's better than that lousy W.A.S.P. band." And you wonder where I get it from, huh?

He also took me to concerts. I know a lot of kids are embarrassed by their parents (and don't get me wrong, they embarrassed me plenty), but I thought it was cool that my dad was interested in what I was getting into. One of my fondest memories was in 1988 when dad took me to see David Lee Roth and Poison in Biloxi, Mississippi. David Lee Roth was touring for his second solo album, *Skyscraper,* and I just had to see this show! Poison, who my dad thought was fun but dumb, opened. David Lee Roth, on the other hand, won my dad over. He was floored by the level of production, which included a huge stage, tons of lights, and Roth singing from a descending boxing ring during "Panama" and on a giant surfboard flying over the crowd during "California Girls." Some guy behind us even spilled his Jack Daniels down my dad's back, to which my dad just said, "Oh well. At least I'll smell like a great time!" It was a memorable, connecting experience, and he left there a fan of David Lee Roth for many years to come.

This level of parental guidance was something I found to be cool. My dad taught me that it wasn't just about the music but also the lyrics. And not just what they were singing about, but what the words meant to me. If a band was singing about getting fucked up and fucking girls or giving their souls to Satan, we talked about it. When I brought home a copy of *At War With Satan* by Venom, he just said, "These guys are pretty good musicians, but the singer is terrible. And son, this Satanic stuff, you know it's all for show right? Oh, and hide that from your mother." My dad was also quick to point out that the misogynistic way some of these bands sang about women was not the way to treat women. My parents trusted me not to take things so literally and encouraged me to ask them when I had questions about subjects I didn't understand. They created a safe space for me to be able to talk about topics that many families wouldn't touch!

Venom was the darkest band I listened to as a kid. They had this demonic, Satanic imagery in their lyrics. When I asked my dad about it, he just reminded me that not everybody believes in the same things religiously and that listening to a band would not possess me with evil spirits or cause me to puke split pea soup. "It's just music, Donald. But if the lyrics are speaking to you and you find yourself questioning things or having questions, ask." So, for a kid attending Catholic school whose mom was an ex-Catholic nun and dad was a former seminary student (those are stories for another day), I guess you can say I was a pretty fucking lucky kid to have such open-minded parents who promoted thinking for yourself.

Dad and I didn't see eye to eye very much and had a lot of clashes over the years. We had very little in common. I was a hopeless dreamer and he was a realist. Dreams were what kept me going and my dad didn't understand that concept. We were different people with different opinions on what success and happiness were. That said, I will always appreciate the fact that we had this connection through music that brought us together and made all the other bullshit, even for a short moment, null and void. Just for the record, I ended up getting that W.A.S.P. album anyway, and to this day, I consider it one of the greatest metal debut albums of all time. Sorry, dad.

RATT N' Roll or pay the toll.
Well, I decided to RATT N' Roll.
Me and RATT guitarist Warren DiMartini.
Atlanta, GA, 2009

I Won a RATT Pack!

People my age will remember a time before the internet, 3,521 cable channels, and cell phones. Back in 1987, we didn't have all the cool shit we have now to entertain ourselves or waste time, but we did have one companion: the radio. That's right! Before FM radio became a stale, pre-programmed series of songs picked by a conglomerate's computer designed to fuel their artist sales, radio was a place where we could hear the songs we loved played by people who shared the same passion for music. That's right, DJs; I'm talking about you. It was also a place where magical things happened, like winning free records, station swag, and concert tickets.

The struggle was real back in the '80s. Do you know how hard it was to be the ninth caller to win something off the radio with a rotary phone? If you were lucky, at some point, your parents upped your chances by getting you your touch-tone phone with redial capabilities. I can't tell you how many hours I spent trying to win tickets to see Mötley Crüe, Ozzy Osbourne, and Sting. Yes, I said Sting. Don't judge me.

In 1987, I was thirteen years old, and like most misfit metal kids my age, my Friday and Saturday nights consisted of me sitting in my room alone. It may sound sad, but honestly, I couldn't have been happier. I had my *Metal Edge, Circus, Faces Rocks*, and *Hit Parader* magazines. I had my own stereo and a kick-ass New Orleans radio station called WRNO. I can still remember the DJs saying, "You are listening to WRNO. We Rock New Orleans!" Get it? How clever is that? Anyway, WRNO had this great DJ who was a metalhead, and his name was Warren. Warren was always playing the cool shit.

One Friday night, I was tuned into Warren's show, and all of a sudden, Warren says, "Be the ninth caller and win tickets to see RATT at the Mississippi Gulf Coast Coliseum!" Biloxi, Mississippi is only about forty-five minutes away from New Orleans, so you bet your ass I was going for this. I grabbed my touch-tone phone and dialed the number. I still remember it. 260-WRNO. I called in and got a busy signal. I called again and still no dice. I hit the redial button one more time and was told to hold. All of a sudden, Warren goes, "WRNO, you're the 9th caller!" I suddenly realize that I hear his voice through the speakers as well. I just let out this loud "WOOHOO!"

I lost my fucking mind. I jumped up and told Warren my name and all that, and he told me to hold on the line so he could get some info from me. I held, and he came back and said, "How old are you?"

"Thirteen years old, sir," I replied.

He laughed and said, "Ok. Well, one of your parents is going to have to come to the studio with you to get these tickets." I hung up the phone, and reality hit me like a two-ton heavy thing. "Fuck. Who is going to take me to this show?"

I broke the news to my folks the next day excitedly by exclaiming, "Mom, Dad! I won a RATT pack." My dad looked up from his cup of coffee and asked me, "What the hell is a rat pack?" I told him, then he looked at my mom and said, "It's your turn!" She took me to the station to claim my tickets, and it turns out that in addition to the tickets, I got a copy of *Dancing Undercover* on vinyl and a tour shirt. Damn, could this get any better? I was the envy of nobody at school, so I didn't have anyone to brag to besides my buddy Mike; but it didn't stop me from being excited. I was on pins and needles every day until the concert weekend arrived.

My mom packed our lunches, and we got in the car and took off for Biloxi. She got a hotel room at a place right next door to the Gulf Coast Coliseum, so all we had to do was walk over. Did I care that my mother was going to be with me at a RATT concert? Are you kidding me? Minnie Mouse could've taken me, and I wouldn't have given a rat's ass (or RATT's ass). I was just so pumped to be seeing RATT in concert finally. We checked in and killed some time by going to visit some friends of my mom's.

We got to the venue right before the doors opened. It was crowded, and people were getting restless, chanting "1-2-3-4, open up the fucking door!" I remember looking up at my mom and her just shaking her head and smiling. There was a long-haired dude in front of us with his girlfriend. He turned around to me and asked, "Is that your mom?"

I said, "Yeah, why?"

He just smiled and said, "You've got a cool mom, lil dude! My mom would never take me to a concert like this. That's cool." Yeah, I thought it was cool as well.

We finally got in, and even though it was a general admission show, we found some killer seats. We were about ten rows up from the stage on the side with a perfect view. The lights went down, and the first opening act was local New Orleans boys, Lillian Axe. I remember thinking it was cool that guys who lived in my neighborhood were on tour opening for RATT, but honestly, I couldn't tell you a single song they played because all I could think about was RATT.

The next band was Queensryche. At the time, I didn't know anything about them. They sounded cool, but they seemed a bit out of place. I knew they were touring for their album *Rage for Order* because they played the song "Walk In The Shadows", and I remember thinking was a cool tune. I wish I could go back to 1987 and tell my younger self that I would eventually love this band and see them live many more times.

Finally, it was time for RATT to take the stage. The house lights went down, and the place erupted in a huge cheer. It sounded like an airplane taking off it was so loud. A good friend once told me that you know you've seen an amazing concert when twenty years later, you can still remember what song that band opened with. That night, RATT opened with the song "Looking for Love" from *Dancing Undercover*. Then Stephen Pearcy yelled, "Welcome to the 1987 *Dancing Undercover* world party!" and slammed into "Wanted Man" from their *Out of the Cellar* album. It was everything I could do to stay in my seat. I loved the sheer deafening volume of the show, and there were more ramps, stairs, and lights on the stage than you can imagine. Plus, a backdrop with a huge RATT logo…just in case you needed to be reminded of who you were seeing.

I remember moments from the show like it was yesterday. Like getting giddy when the band kicked into their hits like "Lay It Down" and "You Think You're Tough." After Bobby Blotzer's drum solo, a six-pack of beer was lowered from the lighting truss to him. He took one out, drank it, and tossed the rest into the front row. After their encore ("Body Talk" and then "Dance," their huge single off of the *Dancing Undercover* album), the house lights came up, and the show was over. It took me a moment to catch my breath and for the ringing in my ears to stop. Mom calmly pulled the cotton out of her ears, smiled at me, and said, "Did you have a good time, honey?" I did because here I am talking about so vividly. I can still feel that rush of excitement as I type this.

Like most bands of their genre, the band's popularity began to decline as the landscape of popular music began to change. In 2002, founding member and guitarist Robbin Crosby passed away from complications of AIDS and a heroin overdose. Inner turmoil in the band put a heavy strain on them, and at one point, two bands were touring under the RATT moniker.

These days, RATT isn't the huge, arena-packing band that they were in the '80s. Maybe it was the change in the musical landscape, or maybe it was the fact that they couldn't keep a consistent lineup. The loss of Crosby seemed to suck the wind out of the sails and any chances of the band reuniting. RATT still hits the road from time to time, playing all the hits that were the soundtrack of my youth while reminding us all to RATT N' Roll or pay the toll.

59

He didn't "Talk Dirty to Me" but he was a super nice guy.
Me & Poison drummer Rikki Rockett.
Atlanta, GA, 2018

Slammin' Glam

Even back in the '80s, glam rock was somewhat taboo. There was this macho mentality within the hard rock/metal community, and it was understood that if you liked glam bands, you were some sort of poseur or a big ol' pussy. I never quite understood, because even though these guys wore makeup, looked like hot chicks (don't even try and tell me you didn't think Poison were hot chicks at first glance), and had some pretty corny lyrics, they still managed to rock the fuck out. But kids who liked Judas Priest and Iron Maiden weren't allowed to like Poison, RATT, or Dokken. I never understood that, because, in my opinion, it was all about the song. If the song was good and I liked it, I couldn't give a rat's ass what they looked like.

Like most kids my age, the first time I heard Poison was their song "Talk Dirty to Me." It was a silly, think-with-your-dick kind of song. Let me tell you, when you're at the age when your female classmates start getting breasts and you're dying to see what's under their shirts, bands like Poison and RATT help you scratch that itch. It was like they were singing about doing all the shit that I couldn't wait to do. I mean, no, I never got to screw three chicks at a time or *"make history in the elevator,"* but hey, they were doing it, and I was like, hell yeah. Tell me all about it.

Even now, there seems to be a huge separation between glam and good ol' jeans and t-shirt Heavy Metal, but I didn't see them that way. I thought of glam bands as extensions of acts like KISS, Alice Cooper, and David Bowie. Ok, I wasn't saying words like "extensions" at age eleven, but you know what I'm getting at—they were a light-hearted approach to the heavy music I loved.

Cranking out some Poison or some Mötley Crüe now and again reminded me that not only was hard rock and metal my favorite music, but it was a multi-faceted genre that could cover all of the emotions I was going through as a kid. When I was pissed off, I had Twisted Sister and Judas Priest. When I felt lost and needed some confidence, I had Dio. And when I just wanted to hear guys singing about banging hot chicks, there was Poison.

There were hard rock bands like Babylon A.D., Tesla, Cinderella, Great White, and Tora Tora whose songs—both lyrically and musically—were at times more substantial than your average glam band. But they got lumped in with the glam scene. Tesla was taking us to school and teaching us about the legendary inventor Nikola Tesla with songs like "Edison's Medicine," Cinderella brought some roots rock to the scene with their *Heartbreak Station* album, Great White wowed us with their blues chops on "House of Broken Love," and Tora Tora delivered the roots-laden hard rock classic (and tragically underappreciated) *Wild America,* which I still believe to be one of the greatest albums of the era.

I think people who are quick to write off glam metal don't get that there was a lot more to it than the make-up and bedazzled spandex. There was some pretty stellar musicianship, substantial lyrics, and some of the best vocalists I've ever heard. Even a band like Poison, who probably went through a case of AquaNet hairspray every night, turned out the beautiful song "Something to Believe In." And Winger? Those guys got beat into the ground, but if you can't listen to "Headed For a Heartbreak" and tell me that's not the best-written ballad of the era, you're just, well, you need to go away. Whatever. Hell, even Gary Holt, the guitar player from Exodus, admitted that even though they used to bash those bands, they coveted the riffs of those like Mötley Crüe, Dokken, and RATT. So if you're one of those people who think glam bands "aren't heavy fucking metal, brah" and that it's all "Cherry Pie," open up, say ah, and be ready to take a pill that may be hard to swallow.

Reading an old copy of *Metal Edge* magazine from the
early '90s with my friend Sebastian Bach on the back.

Read All About It

When I first started listening to hard rock and metal music, magazines were my only source for music news. My family didn't have MTV, and there was no Twitter, Facebook, or YouTube. I'm sure that you youngins can't imagine a life like that. I would save up my allowance, and once a month, I'd skateboard down to the newsstand to pick up *Hit Parader*, *Circus*, and *Faces Rocks*. I'd take them home (stopping at the local Timesaver to pick up a large Icee, a bag of Fritos, and a pack of Garbage Pail Kids), lock myself in my room, and read them from cover to cover. Everything I needed to know about Mötley Crüe, Twisted Sister, RATT, and others was right there at my fingertips, page after page.

As I got older, I started to grow out of *Hit Parader*, and after hearing they were using leftover interviews and even had some fabricated stories, I moved on. In addition to *Circus* and *Faces Rocks*, I got turned on to *RIP Magazine* and *Metal Edge*. *Metal Edge* was awesome because it served multiple purposes. It was like the *National Enquirer* of Heavy Metal, covering the gossip of the glam metal and hard rock scenes—it was how I found out that Vince Neil and Mötley Crüe had parted ways. And their "Rock on the Rise" column tipped you off to up and coming bands while the Concert Calendar gave you the tour dates of your favorite bands. You would scan the list, praying to see your hometown on it, and if you did, you called all your friends to make plans. Finally, when you were done reading it, you could rip the shit out of it and hang posters all over your wall. Trust me. If you were a kid in the mid-late '80s/early '90s, your walls were covered with pictures from *Metal Edge*.

Soon, I got bored reading about which drummer won the reader's poll or what band had the sexiest singer. In 1989, I needed something more substantial. I wanted to go below the surface of these bands, and soon, I found myself reading *RIP Magazine*. The *RIP Magazine* editor, Lonn Friend, and his writers (including Katherine Turman, who would later become a friend, mentor, and editor of this book) truly invested their heart and soul into their work. The interviews were intelligent. None of that "Do you get a lot of groupies?" or "I bet you guys do a lot of blow, don't you?" They would talk about an album's recording process, what inspired songs, and even how they constructed their songs. The articles also often had the writer going deep into the personalities of these musicians, exposing aspects of them that other magazines wouldn't even attempt to do.

The other thing I loved about *RIP Magazine* was that instead of being all glam/hard rock like *Metal Edge* or all thrash like *Metal Maniacs*, *RIP Magazine* would cover everyone from Mötley Crüe and

Guns N' Roses to Megadeth and Slayer. *RIP Magazine* knew no boundaries and boldly took me to places that I may not have gone to myself.

When I started The Great Southern Brainfart blog, my goal as an interviewer was to create a connection with the artists. I do my homework, plan thoughtful questions, try to create a connection with the artist, and I sure as hell don't ask questions like "What's the craziest thing that's happened to you while on tour?" I try to make the most of my time with these artists and to get to the core of what they are all about as people.

Interviewing people such as Dream Theater's Jordan Rudess, Venom Inc's Demolition Man, and Tesla's Jeff Keith not only resulted in great interviews but also great friendships that thrive to this day. Why? I believe it's because I was able to connect with these people on a level that surpassed that of a journalist meeting a musician. I have a sincere interest in these musicians as human beings, more so than untouchable rock stars. *RIP Magazine* inspired me to become the writer that I am today, and for that, I will always be grateful.

Happy 40th Birthday to me! He looked at me like I was nuts. Me & Iron Maiden guitarist Janick Gers. Nashville, TN, 2013

Iron Maiden's Gonna Get You

If you stopped me dead in my tracks and asked me who my all-time favorite band was, I can guarantee, without fail or falter, that I would say Iron Maiden. I mean, with the Grateful Dead running a very, very close second (weird, I know).

Metalheads disagree about who is the biggest and baddest of them all. Some argue it is Judas Priest. Others say it is Dio while some claim it is Motorhead. And I'm sure someone will say that its some shitty ass death metal band I've never heard of whose logo looks like a pile of dead branches. Regardless, I said it when I was twelve, and I'll say it now: Nobody does it bigger or better than Iron Maiden.

The first Iron Maiden album I bought was *Powerslave*. I remember hearing the song "Aces High" at my friend Jimmy's house—this was before he burned all his records to save his soul. His older brother Jay was jamming the album, and I had to hear more. Jay had recorded *Number of the Beast* for me on cassette, but I needed to get *Powerslave*. When I finally saved up enough allowance to buy it, I was blown away. The textured cover, all the subtle details of the elaborate artwork on the front and back—everything about this album drew me in.

Not very long after the purchasing *Powerslave*, Iron Maiden released the double live album *Live After Death*. After another month of hoarding my allowance, I found myself mesmerized while hearing my favorite songs "live." In my opinion, this was—and still is—the greatest live album ever released. From the artwork to the booklet insert to the lyric sheets on each album's sleeve, *Live After Death* had everything. I devoured it (along with Chips Ahoy cookies and milk) sitting on my bed, listening to song after song and reading the lyrics.

There are so many amazing performances on this album. I listened to "Churchill's Speech" so many times that I had it memorized and could talk along with it right before they kicked into "Aces High." Hell, I even recited it during history class in tenth grade for extra credit. "Revelations" made the hair on my arms stand up. There were no cheesy guitar solos, no drum solos; it was just four sides of live Iron Maiden. This was the way Iron Maiden was meant to be heard, and to me, it just didn't get any better than this. I was hooked, and from then on, Iron Maiden was my favorite band (don't worry, Dee, Twisted Sister will always have a spot in my heart).

What I have always loved about Iron Maiden is that while their song lyrics were mature and pretty fucking intelligent, they weren't hard to grasp. It wasn't like listening to a Dream Theater song and needing a fucking dictionary on hand to understand big words. Iron Maiden are storytellers. They are the Bob Dylan of Heavy Metal.

70

With songs based on war history, Egyptian history, literature, and biblical stories, Iron Maiden captured my young imagination and took me away from it all. Iron Maiden created epic journeys for me to embark on with each passing song. Kind of like a "Choose Your Own Adventure" book, but instead of sucking, it ruled my ass hard.

After *Live After Death*, I began working my way backward through the Maiden catalog. Back then, we didn't have the Internet, and I couldn't just go to Wikipedia to look up a band's discography. So, I was kind of all over the place with my digging. I updated my dubbed cassette copy of *Number of the Beast* with the official version. I wore the living fuck out of that cassette, and I eventually bought it on vinyl. Unfortunately, it was permanently borrowed by some fuckhead friend (hence why I refuse to lend out my records even to this day). Next, I bought *Piece of Mind,* and while I loved the artwork and some of the songs, I didn't love that album as a whole (and still don't). But needless to say, Maiden was quickly becoming my obsession, and I needed more.

I don't remember how, but at some point, I learned that Maiden had a singer before Bruce Dickinson named Paul Di'Anno, who did their first two albums. When you're a kid and doing chores for shit pay, you have to be picky about the albums you buy. I decided to start small, so I picked up a cassette copy of *Maiden Japan* for about $5.99. It was a live EP consisting of five songs, and I was blown away. How could the same band have two amazing singers yet sound so very different in their delivery? All I knew was that "Remember Tomorrow" was one of the best songs I had ever heard, and "Innocent Exile" had me doing extra chores to get the money to buy vinyl copies of the first two albums.

The thing that struck me the most about the first two Maiden albums, *Iron Maiden* and *Killers*, is how different they sounded. While it still had their signature sound, it was so raw, so gritty, and so street-sounding. With Bruce Dickinson, Iron Maiden sounded like a refined band. With Di'Anno, they sounded like a bunch of punks who would beat your ass in a back alley after a gig if they saw you heckling them. I loved them both, but I thought of them as separate them from each other.

Don't get me wrong. Iron Maiden isn't perfect. In the last three decades, I have listened to all of the Iron Maiden albums—in order from *Iron Maiden* to *Book of Souls*—many times. It's amazing to me how a band can get so many things right yet so many things wrong, including replacing Bruce Dickinson with former Wolfsbane vocalist Blaze Bayley in 1994. To truly love a band, you also have to call them out on their shortcomings and point out the warts. You don't have to take everything that they offer as gold. If a band puts out a heaping pile of shit like their album *Virtual XI*, you call them out. If they write some terrible fucking songs such as "Weekend Warrior", "Sun and Steel", and "Man on the Edge", you voice your disappointment. That's the point of being a true fan, to care so much that you're willing to stand up and say, "This is shit, fellas. You can do better."

But for all of Iron Maiden's mistakes, they have three times as many triumphs. They have gifted us with a legacy of music spanning over forty years. To this day, the band is still delivering new material, still putting on top-notch performances, and still proving to the world that nobody does it better than Iron Maiden. That is why Iron Maiden fans are tried and true to the death. Up the Irons!

Scorpions: A Band I Always Forget I Love

I always forget about the Scorpions. I don't know why. I mean, "Rock You Like a Hurricane" was on every radio station in the mid-'80s, and I'm pretty sure "Wind of Change" was played at all my high school dances (fuck, who am I kidding? I didn't go to high school dances). My friends and I didn't talk about them except to fight about who had the best Klaus Meine impression—I was definitely the best. "HELLO, EHTLANTAHHHHH! AH YOO VEDDY FAH ZEE BEEGSITTYNIIIIIIIIIIIGHTS?" I guess you'd have to hear it in person to get it, but anyway, the Scorpions were just a band that never made my top bands list. I only own one full Scorpions' album (*World Wide Live*). Why is that?

If I'm honest, I don't *hate* any Scorpions songs. Even the cheesiest of songs like "Tease Me, Please Me," I find myself nodding along to. "The Zoo?" Fucking love it! "No One Like You?" Goddamn,

I'm all over it, and don't get me started on "Big City Nights!" Seriously. They even did a really awesome cover of The Who classic "I Can't Explain" that totally kicked my ass. Their song "Send Me An Angel" from their 1990 *Crazy World* album gives me goosebumps. It's a great example of writing from the heart and producing a beautiful piece of work. And "Wind of Change" captures a real and sincere emotion about their love of Russia. As a songwriter myself, I know songs like this can be personal statements, so even if they come out cheesy, they are still emotions put to music and shared with the world like an open journal.

When I think about it, they were the kings of the ballad, and I usually fucking dread "the ballad." It's generally where a band sounds so contrived and fake, trying to show their soft, emotional side. But with the Scorpions, it's a completely different story. I almost prefer their ballads over their heavy stuff because the songs are so fucking good. I challenge you to take a song like "Still Loving You" and see if any other metal band can do better.

Poison had "fuck me" songs like "Talk Dirty to Me" and "I Want Action." Warrant had tongue-in-cheek songs like "Cherry Pie" and "Love in Stereo." Instead of opting to go in the more cheesy direction of the previously mentioned bands, Scorpions had songs like "Lovedrive," "No One Like You," and "Rhythm of Love" that had a bit of class to them. Goddamn, I challenge anyone to find a song that's as sexy as "Rhythm of Love." That song just oozes passion, and it borders that fine line of a rocker and a ballad. Most of the Scorpions' songs were about the sheer connection between a man and a woman. Even album titles such as *Savage Amusement* and *Animal Magnetism* hinted at that.

Clearly, I like the Scorpions. So, why do I sometimes forget that I do? Even as I type this, "Rock You Like A Hurricane" is playing. I'm smiling and remember Friday nights in my bedroom, eating shitty food and air guitaring to this song. "No One Like You" reminds me of the melodic mastery of this band and "Send Me an Angel" reminds me what an amazingly lyrical band they are:

> *"Wise man said just walk this way To the dawn of the light*
> *The wind will blow into your face As the years pass you by*
> *Hear this voice from deep inside It's the call of your heart*
> *Close your eyes, and you will find Passage out of the dark*
> *Here I am (Here I am) Will you send me an angel*
> *Here I am (Here I am) In the land of the morning star."*

Those lyrics cut me straight to the bone, pierce my heart, and make me feel things very few songs do. It's a good thing I wrote this piece because it serves as a reminder to me that the Scorpions are very much deserving of a seat in my top tier of favorite bands.

School Daze: Me looking thrilled on first day of
school at Mount Zion High School.
Jonesboro, GA, 1989

Where the Fuck is Jonesboro, GA?

I was sitting in my room one Friday night. It was just like any other Friday night: a pack of cupcakes, a glass of milk, headphones blaring some awesome music, and reading a new metal magazine. Then my dad came in to have a talk with me. I didn't know what the fuck was up. As far as I knew, my grades were ok. I hadn't pissed off any teachers, and my mom hadn't yelled at me lately. *What's this going to be about?* I wondered. My dad sat on my bed and said, "Donald, we're going to be moving at the end of the school year."

I was in ninth grade at Archbishop Rummel High School, an all-boys Catholic school in Metairie. Usually, at this point in a kid's life, he has a ton of friends and is well established in a clique of some sort, and to uproot him could be pretty traumatic. For me, I couldn't be fucking happier. I was ecstatic. "Where are we moving to?" I secretly hoped it would be California or someplace cool like that.

"Son, we're moving to Jonesboro, Georgia."

I looked at my dad, and without even thinking, asked, "Where the fuck is Jonesboro, Georgia?" I put my hand over my mouth, but he just laughed. He told me it was a pretty small, rural area only about thirty minutes south of Atlanta.

Atlanta! The very place Mötley Crüe sang about in "Girls Girls Girls"! The place where Bad Company sang, "Oh Atlanta"! I had heard Atlanta was a cool town, and I knew a lot of bands came through there. I was so excited to start a new chapter in my life. New people, new place, new school. I could finally establish my own identity! But when my dad told me I would be going to public high school, I freaked the hell out. In New Orleans, if you were Catholic, I assumed that one only went to public school if you were such a fucking punk that you got kicked out and none of the other hundred Catholic schools would take you. Dad assured me that it was a good school and that I'd be ok.

The only part of the move that would be hard would be leaving the few friends that I had, including a female friend. We'll call her Jan. Jan was a year or so older than me, and she "got me." We weren't dating, but we would spend nearly every Friday or Saturday night talking on the phone long past midnight. When I told her we were moving, she told me that she loved me. I told her that I loved her, and now the thought of leaving was painful. We promised each other that we would keep this thing going long distance, and as soon as I finished high school, I would go back to New Orleans and be with her. Sounds like a fucking power ballad, doesn't it?

When we arrived in Jonesboro, it wasn't what I'd imagined. I figured it would be like fucking hillbilly country, but it was pretty cool. There was a mall, a Waffle House—which I never even heard of—and a cool little corner store down at the foot of our apartment complex where I'd go to buy snacks and the latest metal mag, which they surprisingly carried. My first day of school at Mt. Zion Senior High was nerve-racking. I wore my Cinderella *Night Songs* tour shirt, some ratty looking jeans, and my hair just about grown out past my ears. Terrified, I walked in and surveyed the lunchroom. It didn't take long, but I located a table with three kids with really bad hair, bad skin, and black t-shirts. These were my people. I walked over and asked if I could sit down. They looked at my shirt and said, "Of course, man. Have a seat."

We bonded over how Poison looked ridiculous but was a great band. We agreed that you could enjoy bands like Slayer and Testament and at the same time and dig bands like RATT and W.A.S.P. By the end of lunch, I knew I had found my tribe. This would become my life for the last three years of high school. We went to every fucking show we could go to and loved them all. Poison? Saw them seven times. W.A.S.P., Metallica, Anthrax, Slayer, you name it, we saw it. Hell, we even went to a Winger show, and as much as those guys got ragged on, we all agreed that they kicked fucking ass! The only band we all agreed sucked to no end was Slaughter. What the fuck was that about?

I maintained a friendship with these three dudes, and every now and then, some other dude or two would come over and join in. While it was usually just the four of us, we were very inviting and welcoming. We didn't care what people looked like or what they were into; we just welcomed them into the conversation. Sometimes it would be a jock who wanted to talk about Slayer or a Christian kid wanting to talk about Christian metal like Stryper or Whitecross.

It was just nice to be in a place where I wasn't picked on and ganged up on. Don't get me wrong, I had my confrontations here and there with some mouthy bully, but aside from that, I never felt scared, and I never felt alone. This was a whole new feeling. Another new feeling would be my first heartbreak. After about three months of writing each other letters every week, I noticed that Jan's letters started coming less and less frequently. Finally, she told me she couldn't keep this up and that she had to move on. I must have listened to Winger's "Headed for a Heartbreak" on repeat for a month.

I burned her letters and pictures and threw away everything she ever gave me. I was a living metal power ballad, and it hurt. I had never experienced anything like it, and my dad told me, "Donald, this is your first, and it won't be your last." Looking back on it now, it was a youthful, innocent love, and it makes me wish I hadn't burned those letters—they could have helped me write an epic love ballad to rival the Scorpion's "Still Loving You"—or at least they would've been some sweet nostalgia to look back on and smile.

Saturday Nights at the *Ball*

Back in 1989, every Saturday night from 10:00 p.m. to 1:00 a.m., I found myself planted in front of the television in my bedroom with a hearty supply of snacks, soda, and my remote set to record that night's *Headbanger's Ball* on MTV. When the majority of my high school peers were out getting laid, getting drunk, going to parties, or all of the above, I was at home, ready to tune in to see just what videos host Adam Curry would be playing that night.

As much as I loved attending the *Ball* every weekend, Adam Curry didn't click with me. He didn't seem into it at all. He had this Aqua Net teased long hair, looked completely uncomfortable in his leather jacket and random shirt, and his deadpan face didn't make me feel he was really digging his gig. He looked like someone who didn't really like metal music but was dressed and made to look the part. This usually showed through his lack of enthusiasm and bland "reading off the clipboard" personality. But that all that would all soon change.

In 1990, I heard through the grapevine that Riki Rachtman would be replacing Adam Curry as the host. This was awesome news to me. Riki Rachtman was a cool motherfucker. He was the owner of two of the most bad-ass clubs in Hollywood, The Cathouse and The Bordello. He was roommates with Faster Pussycat singer Taime Downe, and he actually liked hard rock and metal music. I couldn't wait to see how this was going to work, and low and behold, it kicked my ass. Every weekend, I was whisked away on some badass adventure without having to leave my room. It was everything this rock n' roll dreamer could ever want. The videos were cool, but I wanted more. I wanted to see behind the scenes and get to know these bands. Riki did just that, and oh so much more.

Soon *Headbanger's Ball* had a new set and a new logo to go along with the new host who not only looked like a real metal dude but actually *was* a real metal dude. I was always impressed with the endless array of useless information he would share about different bands. Riki was the real deal. It was here that I discovered many of my favorite bands. Bands like Animal Bag, Ugly Kid Joe, Collision, Junkyard, Dangerous Toys, and Rhino Bucket were all bands I saw for the first time on *Headbanger's Ball*.

One night, I remember Riki talking about this new band from Texas that was going to take the metal world by storm. He told us all to stay tuned and to see these guys when they came to our town. That band's name was Pantera, and you want to talk about a facemelt! I remember having a moshpit to the "Cowboys from Hell" video in my room with my kid brother and one of my buddies. Yeah, it was *that* intense. There was just something about the vibe of Riki and the *Ball* that made you want to do shit like that.

Riki used to get a lot of shit for always saying, "This is my favorite band!" about every band he'd play. I loved that about the dude. He never asked for forgiveness, and he never seemed to have a problem loving a band like Skid Row while also being a fan of Slayer, Megadeth, and other thrash bands. This made my friends and I more open to seeking the good in any band and not caring what genre they were. Most kids at my school who were into thrash would totally berate you if you were into anything lighter than Motorhead, yet we had no problem at all digging Slayer, moshing to Megadeth, and admitting that bands like Winger and Slaughter's "Up All Night" was pretty cool fucking song and that Poison actually had some pretty killer tunes.

Headbanger's Ball was where it was at for me. There was no internet back then. There was no YouTube and no cool blogs. All the metal magazines were mostly covering mainstream hard rock/metal bands like Warrant, Mötley Crüe, Metallica, etc., so *Headbanger's Ball* was the best place to discover obscure metal bands, especially if you stuck it through until the last hour. The last hour of the *Ball* was when you'd get some obscure bands like I Love You, My Sister's Machine, Tattoo Rodeo, and even a little band from Seattle called Alice In Chains.

Riki would take me on all these awesome journeys behind the scenes with my favorite bands. He took us backstage and behind the scenes on the *Clash of the Titans* tour, where we got to see live clips and watch interviews with Anthrax, Megadeth, Slayer, and Alice In Chains. One summer, the *Ball* took us behind the curtains and onto the stage of the *Operation: Rock N' Roll* tour with Alice Cooper, Judas

Priest, Motorhead, Dangerous Toys, and Metal Church. These "behind the scenes" episodes were always such an amazing thing for me. I loved seeing how some wild ass singer like Jason McMaster of Dangerous Toys was a really shy, quiet guy or that the guys in Anthrax were really funny and even kind of dorky like me. These episodes brought some of these larger than life bands down to a level where I felt that I could relate to them and not worship them like untouchable gods.

Riki was more than a host. He was the guy that I wanted to be. I wanted to live out those awesome experiences and meet those bands. I wanted to be their buddy, and I wanted to know everything about them. I wanted to drink beer with them, I wanted to hang on the buses, and I wanted to ask them all the questions that nobody else was asking. "What's your favorite junk food on the road?" "If you could sing for any band for just one night, who would it be?" "What album changed your life the most and made you want to be a musician?" These were all questions that I wanted answers to.

As the '90s headed more into the alternative and grunge era, things just started to get weird. *Headbangers Ball* seemed to feature a lot less denim and leather and more flannel and cutoff shorts. Even Riki got his hair cut short and started wearing a flannel around his waist. Oh no. Where was this going? Well, it was plain to see where it was going, and I didn't like it. My interest and connection with *Headbangers Ball* started to die off toward the end, and then eventually, the show was canceled completely. I hung in there, hoping that things would go back to the way they were, but it seemed like the days were long gone. Our time had come, and the torch wasn't even passed. It was completely snuffed out, and the fire was gone.

Years later, I am living out my dreams. I get to interview some of my favorite bands, hang out on tour buses, talk to them on the phone, and take in killer shows. I've interviewed members of Warlock, Queensryche, Tora Tora, and Dangerous Toys, people I watched on *Headbanger's Ball* numerous times. I'm now doing the things I used to dream of as I watched Riki live the dream for me. I learned a lot from Riki. He never seemed to interview these bands. He seemed to talk to them like they were good friends of his, and all the bands really seemed to like him and treat him as one of them.

This was when I knew that I wanted to do something like that when I got older. I didn't want to be one of those guys who just asked a bunch of dull questions and got answers. I wanted to be someone who the bands would allow into their world as an equal. This method seems to have worked well for me, as I've been really lucky to establish some amazing connections and friendships. Being a musician helped me to connect with Dream Theater keyboardist Jordan Rudess, being a big metal dork bonded me with Dangerous Toys vocalist Jason McMaster and Tesla vocalist Jeff Keith, and my undying love and passion for Ronnie James Dio created a tight friendship between myself and longtime Dio guitarist Craig Goldy. Even as I write this, I fight the urge to pinch myself to reassure myself that this is all really happening in my life.

Once I was asked who were my biggest influences as a writer/hard rock journalist. I listed Lonn Friend, Katherine Turman, and Chuck Klosterman. But over the next day or two, I thought about it more and realized that although he isn't a writer, Riki Rachtman made a huge impact on me as a kid and later in my adult life as a writer. How the hell did I let that slip me? Thanks, Riki, and as you always used to say, "Keep one foot in the gutter, one fist in the gold."

Just two Rush fans hanging out.
Me & Bernie Sanders.
Washington DC, 2018

Finding My Way: Making the Connection with Rush

Rush is one of those bands that I find myself loving more and more as I (and they) get older. The first time I ever heard Rush was on that K-Tel compilation *White Hot: Masters of Metal*. When I was a kid, these compilations were awesome because, for one, low price, I could find that I love Dio era Black Sabbath, discover a new (to me) band such as Triumph or Krokus and realize that Slade (even though Quiet Riot covered a couple of their songs) sucked. Anyway, what was I saying?

Oh yeah, *White Hot*. So I picked up this record, and to this day, I vividly remember the needle hitting the groves. Among the metal of Black Sabbath, Krokus, and Quiet Riot was a distinctly different and unique-sounding song. That song was called "Distant Early Warning" by Rush, and I remember thinking that while it didn't sound like metal, I really liked it. As a matter of fact, I *loved* it, and something about that song piqued my little developing 12-year-old rock n' roll brain. I was fascinated that they used keyboards but still sounded heavy. I was so impressed and caught off guard by the time changes in the song (I had just started playing music myself, so I was paying attention to this kind of stuff) and the singer/bassist Geddy Lee's voice. My god, it was so high and kind of weird, but again, something about it clicked with me, and I wanted more. I went and bought *Grace Under Pressure,* but after listening to it, I just didn't get it. The rest of the songs didn't click with me, and I was pretty bummed. I found out that the band had nine fucking albums before this one. Nine! How the hell was I going to know what to listen to?

Maybe Rush was just a little too much for my young self to grasp onto at that time. As the years went by, I found myself being a fan of certain Rush songs that frequented the local rock radio station. "Spirit of Radio," "Fly by Night," "Limelight," "Tom Sawyer," "Working Man," every time I heard them, I loved them, but something kept me from going in all the way. Something kept me from passing through that mysterious door. None of my friends were into Rush, so it wasn't like I had an outlet to ease me into them or to truly allow me to submerge myself into those waters without a lifeline. I couldn't go there on my own, but that would all change in 1989 with the release of an album that altered the way I would look at music forever.

I remember after school one day in 1989 sitting around and doing my homework in front of the TV impatiently awaiting the *Hard 60* on MTV. *The Hard 60* was a daily after-school show on MTV that played sixty minutes of nothing but hard rock and metal. While the usual "hits" of the day like Warrant, White Lion, and Winger would dominate the show, there were always these little diamonds that would shine through, and one of these came in the form of the Rush video for "Show Don't Tell." From the minute that intro kicked in, I can vividly remember stopping everything I was doing. I listened to every single lyric, I watched in awe at these dorky looking guys ripping shit up, and then suddenly, a light went off in the attic of my mind. This is Rush. Is THIS what people were feeling early on that I wasn't? Well, better late to the party than never because from there, I was hooked, and when I picked up the album *Presto*, I was sold. While none of my friends dug this, I couldn't care less. I felt completely moved by this album. Maybe a year later, Rush released their compilation, *Chronicles*, and it was there that the doors opened for me. *Chronicles* was (and is) a perfect mix of songs spanning Rush's long career that was easy for me to digest, allowing me to dip my toes into those progressive complex waters.

The waters of this progressive ocean seemed to be kind of scary and intimidating, but this collection of songs made me feel less overwhelmed. But it only took one, *one* song, to truly captivate me. That song was "Subdivisions":

> *"Subdivisions. In the high school halls*
> *In the shopping malls. Conform or be cast out."*

When my 17-year-old head processed those very words, I found myself crying because much like Twisted Sister and Dio, somebody out there knew exactly what I was going through. Those very words stuck to me like glue, and the connection was made. From that point on, Rush would continue to be a part of my life, but for one reason or another, they would fade to the background as life changed in many ways. My musical tastes grew and evolved over the twenty-eight or so years since I had first laid ears on them. Rush was never far behind me, and they were always there for me when I needed them, but not until 2013 did they make a huge return to the forefront of my life.

In 2013, I picked up the DVD for Rush's *Clockwork Angels* tour, and as I settled in to watch it, the opening song "Subdivisions" filled the room, and a chill went down my spine. The hairs on my arm stood at full attention, and I immediately felt a tear run down my face. There they were. Rush had come full circle and found their way back to me. It was just like running into an old friend where, even though you haven't seen them in many years, it was like no time had passed. In song after song, it was like we were catching up on lost time, reminiscing about the old days, and reconnecting a friendship that had somewhat faded yet never fully gone away, even after almost thirty years.

It's been great having Rush back and playing such a big part in my life again. Not only have I been digging those songs that I loved so much all these years, but I'm also completely loving the fact that I am connecting to aspects of Rush that I just never vibed with, even early on. There's something truly magical and special about finding a connection like that. It's like opening a door to a room you never knew existed in a house that you've lived in all your life. This is an exciting time for me to be a Rush fan because these days, I have friends who share my love for this band and can serve as not only guides but as partners in my journey deep into the complex, intricate, and exciting world known as Rush.

Remembering
Operation: Rock N' Roll

It was the summer of 1991. I was preparing to go into my senior year of high school. Hard Rock/Metal music was still reigning supreme and dominating MTV and in political news, the Gulf War had finally come to an end in August of that year. In honor of the US troops involved in Operation: Desert Storm, the *Operation: Rock & Roll* tour was assembled. The press conference to announce the tour even had Judas Priest vocalist Rob Halford and Alice Cooper riding down the streets of Phoenix, Arizona in a tank.

The news of this tour had me pumped behind belief. As if Alice Cooper AND Judas Priest together on the same bill wasn't enough, Metal Church, Dangerous Toys, and Motorhead were also a part of this mind-blowing lineup. I was beside myself with excitement. I started saving money right away for a ticket and t-shirts (yes, plural). I was more excited about this show than I was for

Clash of the Titans tour took place a couple of weeks prior featuring Slayer, Megadeth, Anthrax, & Alice in Chains. And I didn't know it at the time, but *Operation: Rock & Roll* would also be Rob Halford's last tour with Judas Priest until he would return to the band in 2003.

What I remember the most about this show was that it was hotter than hell that day. Atlanta in the summer is downright miserable, and black is not the best color shirt to wear, but regardless, Lakewood Amphitheater was an ocean of black t-shirts, pale skin, and long hair. My buddy and I were running a bit late because of having to take public transportation, but we got there just as Metal Church was taking the stage. Metal Church had just put out an album called The Human Factor, and they were experiencing some minor success due to a video on *Headbanger's Ball* called "A Date With Poverty." I remember being so impressed with their set and their singer, Mike Rowe.

Even to a 1/3 full amphitheater, Mike and Metal Church played like that place was sold out with tons of energy. They blew me away, and to this day, The Human Factor is one of my favorite metal albums that have stood the test of time very well. After their awesome set, we immediately made our way to the merch booth to get our swag. I was super pumped to purchase a new Dangerous Toys tour shirt along with an Alice Cooper one as well. My buddy opted for the Judas Priest and Motorhead combo, so between the two of us, we pretty much supported all the bands sans Metal Church. Hey, at least we watched their set.

Dangerous Toys was up next, and they were supporting their second album, *Hellacious Acres*. This was a band that I loved the moment I heard their debut single, "Teas'n Pleas'n." I had seen them on their first tour with Junkyard, and I was ecstatic to see part of this amazing bill. It was really cool seeing Dangerous Toys on a huge stage. The band had this huge backdrop that looked like the album cover, and the amps were covered by smaller backdrops of that creepy ass clown mascot.

Dangerous Toys came out to a nearly full amphitheater, and I could tell that these guys were going to kick ass and take names. At this point, they had quite a bit of buzz to them and already had a great reputation for putting on an amazing live show. Their set was way too short, but damn were they awesome. They opened with "Sport'n a Woody" from their debut album and managed to cram in hits like "Scared" and "Teas'n Pleas'n" along with a few deep cuts from the Hellacious Acres album. They were so fucking good, and the crowd's reaction was great. I thought for sure they'd return soon enough as arena headliners. Yes, I thought they were that good, but unfortunately, it wasn't meant to be.

Motorhead came up next, and at this point, I had never seen Motorhead live before. I was so pumped to see them as I really loved their *1916* album and was a proud owner of *No Sleep Till Hammersmith* on vinyl. The band came out opening with "Dr. Rock", and my first impression was that they were so fucking loud it was nearly painful. I could literally feel my chest rumbling from the bass, and the sheer volume of it made my ears hurt. I managed to scoot out to the bathroom and get some tissue to put in my ears so it wouldn't be so damn loud. Once I got back to my seat, I was fine and totally loving every note they played. The audience was so into them that you would've thought they were one of the headliners. Their set was full of great songs new and old such as "No Voices In The Sky," "R.A.M.O.N.E.S," and "Ace of Spades." Lemmy didn't do a lot of talking. He's a man of few words, so he opted to kick all our asses, melt our faces, and then say good night. The fact that there were still two huge acts left to play blew my mind.

At this point, my buddy and I were going head to head. I was there to see Alice Cooper, and he was there for Judas Priest. He was convinced that Priest would reign supreme, but I was sure Cooper would wipe his ass with Priest. The end result? BOTH FUCKING WON! How can you go wrong with a dual headliner of Alice Cooper and Judas Priest? Alice had this awesome stage show with a huge skull, hands on each side of the stage holding the drums and the keyboards with everyone else in the middle. Alice's set started with a bang opening with "Under My Wheels" and went on to deliver the best Alice show I had seen up to this point.

I remember "Go To Hell" being the highlight of the show. Alice walked through this screen and became part of some footage that was playing where he was being tortured in this thing that looked like a cross between a dentist chair and an electric chair. Finally, Alice broke free and ran toward the screen, and when he finally got right up to the screen, he broke through it and was back on stage just in time to end the song. Alice's performance was stellar, and his band was top-notch awesome. Sprinkled among the classic hits, Alice had to squeeze in some newer (now classic) tracks like "Trash," "Poison," and "Hey Stoopid." Alice closed the night with "Elected," which had everyone rooting for the Wild Party, of which Alice Cooper will always remain president. I could've easily used another hour of Alice, but all in all, this was a flawless performance.

Finally, it was time to see what Judas Priest was going to bring to the stage. Following Alice Cooper isn't an easy thing to do, but Judas Priest, in their own right, kicked a lot of ass. Priest opened their set with "Hell Bent For Leather," which had vocalist Rob

Halford riding out from under the drum riser on his Harley, and the band just slayed that tune. Priest's setlist was off the charts with hits like "Heading Out to the Highway," "Metal Gods," and "The Ripper," but it was the pre-encore of "The Green Manalishi" that was the real show stopper for me.

Priest closed out in true "hits" fashion with "Breaking the Law," "Living After Midnight," and "You've Got Another Thing Comin'." As Priest left the stage, I clearly remember thinking that while Alice was still my favorite of the night, having Priest and Cooper on the same bill was lightning in a bottle. Looking back on this show now, I feel that even then, I knew that I saw something that was amazing. The fact that I saw all of these amazing acts on one stage together was an amazing thing, and all that for under twenty bucks? Hell, these days, a show like that would cost over one-hundred bucks easily. *Operation Rock & Roll* is one of those moments in my life where it was great to be a teenager and great to be lucky enough to see so much great music in one day on one stage for a low price. Those were the days.

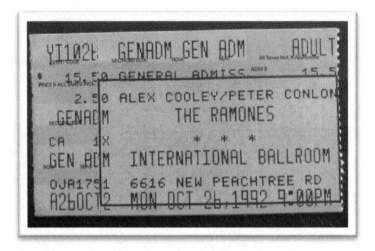

One of the most physically brutal shows I
have ever been to in my life. I'm still pissed
about losing my spot against the barricade.

Murder in the Front Row

You can only begin to imagine the level of excitement that comes with being in the front row of a show by your favorite band. I'm not talking about front row seats at some posh, air-conditioned theater where you're taking in a nice evening of music. I'm talking about general admission, standing room only shows, where you cue up in line at 3:00 p.m. when the doors to the shitty, armpit, taint of a club don't open until 7:00 p.m.

If you've been there, you know what I'm talking about. I've been there many times in my youth. The doors open, and you run faster than you ever have to secure your spot right up front. It's also important to make sure you're on the correct side of the stage for the band you're seeing. For instance, if you're going to see GWAR and you want to be on Balsac the Jaws of Death's side, you need to be pressed up against the front of the right side of the stage. If you're going to see Megadeth and want to heckle Dave Mustaine with hopes that he'll say something witty and toss your ass out, you need to be stage center. Get it?

Countless times in my youth, I was that person. I needed to be upfront for every fucking show I went to. Faster Pussycat, Ugly Kid Joe, Saigon Kick, Testament, Exodus, GWAR... I wanted to be right up there on the front line. The weight of anywhere from 300 to 1000 people pushing into you as you brace yourself against the barricades, praying you won't crack or break a rib. The feeling of not being able to breathe or move an inch even if you tried, getting booted in the head by a Doc Marten wearing crowd surfer, getting beer thrown on you—and loving every minute of it—was something that made up a huge bit of my concert experience.

There is a certain kind of magic and energy that takes place right up against the stage. Unless you've lived it, you probably wouldn't understand. But I'm sure it's the same case whether you're seeing a pop band, a country artist, or your favorite metal band. There's this connection with the group that you just don't get from being far away. Locking eyes with the singer and having him or her put the mic in your face to sing, fist-bumping the bassist, getting a pick from the guitarist. Just being a part of the fuel that adds to the fire. You help the band give the very best show they can give to the rest of the room.

I've had some great times upfront, and I've had some pretty harsh and brutal times, too. I got a black eye while at a Dangerous Toys and Junkyard show. I got booted in the head by a crowd surfer while seeing NOFX. I got my leg peed on (yes, real piss) while upfront at a Black Crowes show. But the worst thing ever was completely being robbed of my front row spot at a Ramones show in 1992.

The Ramones were playing the International Ballroom in Atlanta, Georgia. The band was touring for their *Mondo Bizzaro* album. I remember it like it was yesterday. They were touring with some shitty fucking band called Overwhelming Colorfast and Social Distortion (who I was actually looking forward to seeing). A couple friends and I arrived at the venue at two in the afternoon, and we were easily the fifth, sixth, and seventh people in line. We were destined to be right up in front of Joey Ramone. Nothing was going to stop us.

As the hours passed, the line got longer and longer, and the minute the doors opened, we booked it across the huge-ass warehouse and secured our places against the barricade, front, and center as planned. We were pumped as fuck because there we were, front and center, right where Joey Ramone would be. The first band, Overwhelming Colorfast, went on, and everyone pretty much just stood with their arms folded. Try to picture that kid in *Spinal Tap* who's sitting down and giving them a thumbs down during "Jazz Odyssey." That was everyone in the room.

The next band up was Social Distortion. Social Distortion is this great band that mixes rockabilly, punk rock, and '50s tinged rock n' roll. They had such a unique sound for the time, and I loved what they were doing. I had never seen them before, but I had their album, *Somewhere Between Heaven and Hell*, so I was pumped to see them. They came out and opened with "Cold Feelings," and all of a sudden, things got just a bit rougher. The crowd was pushing. I could feel my chest getting tight, but the three of us stuck together and held our own. By the end of their set, I was exhausted, but we had made it. The Ramones were next, and Joey Ramone was going to be right in front of me. They came out after their traditional "The Good, The Bad, & The Ugly" taped intro and slammed into "Durango 95." This was when shit started to get real.

I literally could feel my ribs pressed up against the barricade, I could barely breathe, and I was loving it. I was holding on for dear life when suddenly, I saw my two buddies get swept out of their front row positions like someone being dragged out to sea by a powerful current. I held my ground until the chant of "LOBOTOMY! LOBOTOMY!" started for "Teenage Lobotomy." As the band kicked, people behind me literally lifted my fat ass off the ground and flipped me over the barricade. What does this mean, you ask? Well, when this happens, security escorts you to the end of the barricade and to the back of the International Ballroom you go… unless you want to fight your way back upfront.

Eventually my buddies ended up with me at the back of the room, and by the time we collected ourselves, the Ramones were on their seventh song. We looked like we had just been roughed up by a major league football team. We laughed it off and continued to stand in the back where it was safe and roomy, and we enjoyed my all-time favorite Ramones show. After that show, I started to give up my place in the front row to a newer generation of people to experience and live.

Every now and then, if it's a small, sparsely attended club show, I'll be right up front banging it out with the band. But these days you can find me in the "dad section" at the back of the club. Me and a friend hanging back, drinking a cold PBR or Miller Lite tallboy, enjoying the show, and appreciating those folks upfront. I know what it's like up there. It's exciting, it's painful, and it's fun as all fuck. I also know that it's those kids getting "murdered" in the front row while the band plays who are setting the tone, giving the band the energy and drive to put on the best fucking show they can for those of us in the back who once braved the front row like they are. We may be older and hanging in the back, but it doesn't make us lesser fans. We just prefer to get home after a concert without a cracked rib, bloody nose, or someone else's piss on our jeans.

Caught in a Dream. Me & Alice Cooper.
Atlanta, GA, 2015

Pleased to Meet You, Alice Cooper

My connection with Alice Cooper goes back to 1986. I was twelve years old, and I had heard some of Alice's already classic songs on the radio like "School's Out," "Billion Dollar Babies," and "Under My Wheels," and I thought they were fucking killer songs. They sounded "classic" to my young ears but at the same time just as cool, if not cooler, than the more modern stuff I was listening to. I didn't know much about Alice Cooper, and since this was long, long before the internet, I had to ask someone who would know more: my dad. My dad was not really a rock n' roller—he loved folk and Americana music—but I figured he'd know who Alice Cooper was since Alice was old and my dad was old. When I asked him, I remember him just smiling and saying, "Donald, Alice Cooper was a freak! He put on crazy live shows with snakes and all kinds of props, but he had some good songs." A few nights later, my dad came home from work and said, "Donald, I bought this for you. Let's put it on." It was a copy of Alice Cooper's *Greatest Hits*. We sat in my room and put on the record. As "I'm Eighteen" blasted through the speakers, I remember feeling so moved by it. It wasn't W.A.S.P, it wasn't Mötley Crüe, and it wasn't Iron Maiden, but it was heavy in its own way. The music sounded gritty, nasty, and full of attitude. I loved what I was hearing.

My dad went on to explain to me just how crazy Alice Cooper's music sounded in the '70s. He told me it was a time where music was so homogenized, safe, and fluffy. Bands like Fleetwood Mac, Bread, and the Bee Gees had little to no substance, and while his peers were sugarcoating and glazing life, Alice was showing the dirty reality. He explained that Alice was like the homeless guy you passed on the street trying to pretend you didn't see him, even though you know he's there. That's some pretty heavy shit for a twelve-year-old to be told by his dad. Yeah, my dad could be pretty intense at times.

Soon Alice became a trusty companion. Like Iron Maiden and Dio, Alice's songs helped me escape when life got hard. I became a guest in Alice's various worlds, getting away from the outside "real" world that was such a fucking hassle. Getting bullied, getting made fun of for the music I love, and just feeling the oppression of society in general was something I longed to get away from. Listening to Alice, I could be a guest (or more appropriately, a spider on the wall) in his nightmare, I could be an outlaw on the run, or I could live in a political world where the only party that mattered was the "wild" party.

Even when my life got better, Alice was still around. Sometimes literally—I never had to wait long to see an Alice Cooper show! An Alice Cooper concert was (and still remains) an unforgettable, fun experience. In all honesty, Alice is one of the few acts whose music is as mesmerizing and mind-blowing as his over-the-top visually stunning live performances. Since 1990, I have seen nine Alice Cooper shows. Every time I would see Alice live, I would go home and wish that I could have the opportunity to meet him and thank him for all the years of timeless music that got me through some rough years. Well, a dear friend who has connections to Alice made that wish come true and got me and my wife Lizzi tickets to the show along with backstage passes.

The show was in Atlanta at Phillips Arena on August 30, 2015. It was a co-headlining show with Mötley Crüe with Alice going on first. After Alice's stellar performance, we got in line with a handful of others to go backstage and meet him (bonus: that meant we escaped having to sit through Mötley Crüe). I stood there in silence, trying to figure out what I was going to say to Alice Cooper. You know that scene in *The Godfather*, where Luca Brasi is rehearsing what to say to the Godfather on the day of his daughter's wedding. That was me. "Alice, it's such an honor to meet you." "Alice, thank you for…" Then suddenly, it was my turn.

As I approached him, Alice reached his hand out and said, "And what's your name?"

With my mouth gaping, I stuttered out "uh, Don."

Alice laughed and said, "It's ok. Breathe."

I just let out a laugh, and I said, "Alice, thank you so much for all the music. I'm sure you've heard this lot, but your music really got me through a pretty rough childhood."

He smiled and said, "Don, thank you for saying that. That really means a lot to me. Let's take some pictures, and I'll sign your albums. Oh, wow, you still have all the inserts for *Billion Dollar*

Babies!" I was speechless, and if you know me, you'll know that me being speechless is a very rare occurrence.

While I was trying to collect myself, he looked to my wife Lizzi and said, "And who is this beautiful lady?" He then went on to have a really sweet conversation with her asking her what she did and telling her about how his wife was actually a part of his show. Lizzi found him charming and such a nice person. I told Alice about how my dad bought me *Greatest Hits* and that this was what started it all. When I told him my dad had passed away, he was so sympathetic and said, "I'm sorry for your loss." Alice was every bit as nice as I hoped he would be and then some. He has a way of making you feel like you are the only person in the room by giving you his undivided attention. My wife still talks about how awesome it was to meet him and what a nice guy he was.

I consider myself a lucky guy. Over the years, I've had some amazing opportunities to interview and hang out with some of my all-time favorite hard rock/metal bands. But having the opportunity to have five minutes with Alice Cooper is something I will never forget. Getting the chance to thank him for all the years of music that continues to be a huge part of my life and to see his reaction to those words will last me a lifetime.

Hey man, I think I like being scared and I wish you
all were there. Me & Dangerous Toys.
Atlanta, GA, 2019

Take it Sleazy

Hard rock music in the late '80s/early '90s was, well, a bit on the pretty side. I don't mean that in any disrespect because I liked a lot of these bands. But bands like Poison, Warrant, Winger, and hell, even KISS seemed to put so much emphasis on their image, forcing the music to play second fiddle. With their perfect teeth, flawless hair, and thin bodies, the girls just loved them, and it left us ugly guys wondering, "What about us?"

I knew I had no chance with the chicks. I had horrible hair, bad skin, and I was far from cool. But of a sudden, a whole new breed of bands started to surface—bands that were homely looking, the antithesis of what those pretty bands were all about. Hell, some of these guys were downright fucking ugly, and I absolutely loved it. If bands like Poison and RATT were talking about getting in fights and fucking chicks, bands like Junkyard and Circus of Power were the guys sitting at the back of the bar watching it all happen while they drank, more than content to take it in than to participate.

These dirtbag-style bands were another facet of the hard rock/metal world that struck a chord with me, and I loved it. Sleaze rock is what they called it, and it couldn't have had a better tag attached to it. To me, four bands did it better than any of them: Dangerous Toys, Circus of Power, Rhino Bucket, and Junkyard. I fucking loved these bands. I loved that the gritty, bluesy influence behind the music, I loved the lyrics that spoke of the seediness of living in the underbelly of rock n' roll, and most of all, I just loved the fucking attitude.

In 1990 when I was in 10th grade, two of my favorite bands, Dangerous Toys and Junkyard, made their way to Atlanta to play at Center Stage Theater. I was absolutely beside myself. I was so fucking pumped that two of my favorites were playing in my town. Both were rising to the top like curdled cream in coffee, as each band had pretty popular songs that got frequent play on MTV. Dangerous Toys had "Teas'n Pleas'n" and Junkyard had "Hollywood."

The show was outstanding. Dangerous Toys were every bit as awesome as I hoped they would be and then some. Hearing all my favorite songs like "Sport'n a Woody," "Queen of the Nile," and "Scared," to name a few, was mind-blowing. The band was so full of fire, energy, and tattoos. There was something magical about their set that makes me remember it like it was yesterday. Jason McMaster was a frontman that could give any of the greats a run for their money. After the closing song, "Teas'n Pleas'n," McMaster took off one of his bracelets and handed it to me. I wore that fucking bracelet all through high school until I let this girl that I liked my senior year wear it. She never gave it back, but hey, at least I got to tell McMaster that story in an interview, which he seemed to find quite amusing.

I believe that sleaze rock as we know it began with AC/DC and Bon Scott. "Shot Down in Flames," "Beating Around the Bush," "Prowler," and "It's a Long Way to the Top if You Wanna Rock N' Roll" are just a few examples of where I believe AC/DC pioneered the sleaze movement. Then there was early Mötley Crüe and Hanoi Rocks, two bands who looked glam but played sleaze.

Rhino Bucket embodied the vibe of sleaze rock in the '90s. They had that Bon Scott-era AC/DC vibe to them and again, they looked like hell. I mean, these guys looked like they had just left their shifts at Jiffy Lube and rolled up to the gig and jumped on stage.

Slik Toxik came in at the end of the sleaze movement. They kind of looked like Skid Row as in that they were a bunch of rough-looking dudes who didn't give a fuck. They had songs like "Big Fucking Deal," "Sweet Asylum," and "It's Not Easy" that took that sleaze sound to a whole new level, infusing a bit of Heavy Metal into it, which really scratched an itch for me. I had such high hopes for Slik Toxik; I felt they very much could've been one of the bands to keep the ship afloat. Unfortunately, even the sleaze was no match for the flannel, and much like many of the other bands, they stepped back into the shadows and disappeared from sight, leaving a big ol' Dirty Sanchez under the nose of rock n' roll.

However, much like traditional metal, sleaze rock seems to be having a renaissance. Bands like Kickin' Valentina, Santa Cruz, Hardcore Superstar, and Crash Diet all reached back to their sleaze roots and found a way to put a modern spin on this classic root genre. Much like how bands like Holy Grail and 3 Inches of Blood took the classic, traditional metal and put their own spin on it, these bands are doing the same thing for sleaze rock.

This sleazy rock revival has started to bring back a lot of the greats from back in the day. Faster Pussycat, Rhino Bucket, Junkyard, Little Caesar, and even Dangerous Toys have returned to the stage and found themselves putting out new material and hitting the road, playing to packed venues to both nostalgic older fans and newer fans who weren't even alive when these bands were in their youthful prime. While I might not love it all, I do love that these bands are coming back and doing so with a bang.

Maybe it's just the right time for this music to make a comeback. In these times when the political and social climate is so overbearing and depressing, it's just nice to have some good old sleazy rock and roll to entertain us and remind us that no matter what's going on in the world, we can still, even just for a moment, forget about it all and have some ridiculously sleazy fun.

Me & my good friend Tesla
vocalist Jeff Keith.
Atlanta, GA, 2019

Me presenting Cinderella lead
singer/guitarist Tom Keifer with the
essay you're about to read.
Atlanta, GA 2019

...But Are They As Good As Tesla & Cinderella?

One hot summer day back in 1989, I was thumbing through the local free paper when I saw an ad for one of my favorite bands: Tesla. They were playing at the Fox Theater with Great White and Kix. I just *had* to go. The problem was that I had no friends to go with (we had just moved to Georgia, and school hadn't started), so my dad reluctantly stepped up to the plate and got us balcony tickets for the show.

Tesla was a special band to me. I absolutely loved their debut album, *Mechanical Resonance*, because it was just so different. It wasn't the slick, polished, makeup-clad glam rock that was ruling the airwaves and MTV at the time. Tesla was this little band from California with a huge sound that was more reminiscent of backyard BBQs, bonfire parties, and good old gnarly, gritty rock and roll with a Heavy Metal twist. As much as I loved the debut when the band released *The Great Radio Controversy*, I was over the moon. Track one, "Hang Tough," has a great mellow breakdown after the lead guitar solo that still gives me goosebumps every time I hear it. The dynamics on this album were something that I hadn't heard a lot of, if at all. Tesla had elements of the greatest metal guitar duos-- shredding licks and picking notes out of the sky—but then they'd bring it down with acoustics and a more melodic approach on songs like "Love Song" and "The Way it Is." All I knew was that this band was something special and I had to see them live.

On July 30, 1989, my dad and I rolled up to the Fox Theater for the show and made our way up to our seats. My dad bought an overpriced beer (which I bet back then was like six bucks), and he bought me a Coke. We were both blown away by the beauty of the Fox Theater. I had never seen anything like it in my entire life. The opening band, Kix, took the stage, and my dad pretty much made fun of them the whole time. I thought they were just ok. I can't remember who opened or closed the show, just that Great White and Tesla were co-headlining. What I do remember is that Great White was really good, but when Tesla hit the stage, I was blown out of the back of the theater.

Tesla came out, guns blazing, with "Lady Luck" from *The Great Radio Controversy*, and before I could even get my last cheer out, they were going straight into "Hang Tough." I was so excited I just lost my mind. I looked over at my dad, clad in a Hawaiian shirt and shorts and cotton stuffed in his ears, and he smiled and gave me a thumbs up. I can remember it as plain as day when Tesla began "Gettin' Better." My dad leaned into me and said, "This is probably the best band I've ever seen in concert. These boys are fantastic." I was so psyched that he was enjoying himself. He told me later that he loved the fact that not only were they great performers but that they had a lot of different ways of presenting their music. After they played "Modern Day Cowboy," he said to me, "I doubt any band could do a better job than this."

Just a few months later and two days shy of my birthday, I still didn't have any friends that I felt comfortable going to shows with. On September 3rd, my dad once again seized the opportunity to take my kid brother and me to see Cinderella, White Lion, Warrant, and Tangier at Lakewood Amphitheater. I was so excited because the last time I had seen Cinderella was as the opening act for Judas Priest a year or so before. To see them as headliners were going to be a thrill.

My dad critiqued each of the bands. First up was Tangier. I had never heard them and thought they were great, definitely a Cinderella type of band with their blues-infused hard rock. My dad commented, "These guys are really good. Their singer looks older than the other guys, but what a voice. I really like these guys. These guys rock. They should have played longer." Bill Mattson, former Tangier vocalist, if you're reading this, please take this as a huge compliment from one of the grumpiest motherfuckers I have ever known.

My dad's snarky attitude made an appearance as Warrant took the stage. My dad said he thought that they were just flat out stupid and even went as far as to say that they made Poison look like MENSA members. He said, "Is 'fuck' the only word this guy knows? He must talk so much because their music is so terrible." He summed up their set with "The announcer called them 'the horniest band in the world'? More like the worst band in the world. These guys will never make it."

It didn't get much better when White Lion came on. My dad said he thought they had great stage presence but that Mike Tramp was a "tone-deaf Fabio." "That guitar player is fabulous, " he commented about Vito Bratta. "Why is he wasting his time in this crappy band? These guys are not much better than Warrant." When they covered "Radar Love" by Golden Earring, my dad said, "Wow, I thought I hated that song before, now I hate it even more."

At this point, I was starting to get nervous about what he'd think of Cinderella, but because he loved Tesla so much, I knew that he would dig them. Cinderella began their set with "Bad Seamstress Blues" and "Falling Apart at the Seams," and when it kicked in, a curtain dropped, exposing a huge stage full of stairs, ramps, and lights. My dad looked over at me and said, "Now, this is some good stuff." Cinderella played a great selection of material from their two albums as I'd hoped, and my dad was really enjoying himself. "Night Songs" was a big hit with him as he said that it reminded him of vampires.

When Cinderella went into "Don't Know What You Got (Till It's Gone)," Tom Keifer descended from the lighting truss on a white baby grand piano. Dad thought this was one of the coolest things he had ever seen, asking me wonderingly, "How can they top this?" He loved "Coming Home" and "Gypsy Road." He told me he thought "Shake Me" was a pretty silly song but that it was still enjoyable. During "Shake Me," these three girls were standing on their seats in front of us. They all lifted their shirts, flashing their bare breasts at the band. My dad looked at them, looked at me, and said, "Your mother doesn't need to know every detail of what went on here, ok?" and sipped his overpriced draft beer. Score 1 for pops!

When Cinderella returned for their encore of "Long Cold Winter," artificial snow, bathed in purple lights, fell from the covered area of the amphitheater. The band delivered what is still my favorite Cinderella show to date. My dad's mouth was open with astonishment. He was so fixated on the music, the snow, and the band that he didn't say a word until after the song was over. When it was over, he proclaimed, "Now THAT is something that I don't think anyone could ever top. That was one of the most beautiful things I have ever seen."

From then on, whenever I came home from a show, my dad would ask, "So how was the show?" And if I said it was awesome, he would quickly reply "Yeah, but were they as good as Tesla and Cinderella?"

Before my father passed away in 2012, he had to spend some time in the hospital, which gave us time to talk and reminisce, including about those shows. He was so impressed that both bands were still around. I wish he could've lived long enough to see me interview Tom Keifer twice and to eventually become very close friends with Jeff Keith of Tesla.

I saw Tesla recently, and while sitting backstage with Jeff Keith, I told him this story. When I finished, he let out the heartiest of laughs and said, "Don buddy, I bet you anything your dad is with us right now." I smiled for a brief moment. I liked the thought of him being there, grinning with pride that I was hanging out with one of the bands he thought to be the best of the best and that they seemed to respect me and what I do as much as I respect them.

Rockin' the bedroom. Rehearsing with Gutterslut.
Jonesboro, GA, 1991

Start Your Own Damn Band:
Part 1: Gutterslut

When I moved to Jonesboro, Georgia from New Orleans in 1989, I had only been playing guitar for about three years. I hadn't been in a band, but I had made some music with my buddy Mike, who played drums from time to time. We called ourselves Skeleton Crue. Get it? The Stephen King novel meets Mötley Crüe? I think we learned how to play "I Won't Forget You" by Poison and maybe a RATT song? Yeah, it was about as good as you'd imagine. At my new school in Jonesboro, Georgia, it seemed that everyone played the guitar, and they were all so much better than me. I wasn't confident enough to get out there and jam with others, so I just holed up in my room and practiced playing while blasting my albums (sorry Mom).

I wanted nothing more than to have a band. I knew I wasn't good enough to play Iron Maiden or shit like that, but I could play the fuck out of AC/DC and The Ramones. I mean, the songs were usually four chords, and even I could pull that off. I just needed to find other kids to fulfill my vision. I ended up befriending a guy who decided he wanted to be a drummer. He had never played before, but I was like, sure, why not. His mom got him a cheap set of drums, and we began playing in his garage.

We would spend most Saturdays just jamming on songs that I knew how to play on guitar. I couldn't play them well at all but had a blast knocking out songs like, "Same Old Song and Dance" by Aerosmith, "For Whom the Bell Tolls" by Metallica, and "Highway to Hell" by AC/DC. We were having fun but we both decided we wanted to take things to another level.

We knew we needed a vocalist. We were friends with this tall, lanky, blond-haired kid, and we were like, "Hey man, wanna sing in our band?" He had never sung in a band, and he was like, "Sure, I'll give it a shot." He wasn't too bad and could actually carry a tune, but what I liked most was his confidence and his willingness to try things. This inspired me, and I dug that.

We had a bassist, but he unexpectedly quit after two rehearsals, so we decided that we would be a bass-less band. Fuck it. Who needs a bassist? What we did need was a name. I'm not sure how we came up with it, but somehow, we settled on Gutterslut. You can only imagine how proud our parents were. We practiced any song that didn't require me moving past the fourth or fifth fret of my guitar, and for better or for worse, eventually, we started writing our own songs. We weren't good enough to be a metal band, and with our limited musical skills and obnoxious teenage mentality, we were closest to a fledgling punk band.

If you heard the titles of some of our songs, you'd swear we were huge Anal Cunt fans, only none of us ever listened to Anal

Cunt. We had a song called "I Hate Red," about this traffic light by our drummer's house that always seemed to stay red. Another one of our songs was called "Ah Man" and was about this asshole kid who used to bum cigarettes off of me and permanently "borrow" albums from me. Whenever I'd refuse to give him a cigarette or lend him an album, he'd go, "ah man, c'mon!" Looking back on it, the lyrics to this song were ridiculous and kind of mean, but they reflected my sixteen-year-old mentality perfectly:

> *"You're a fat ass smelly bum.*
> *Get out of our way cuz here we come.*
> *We'll run you over, and we'll knock you down.*
> *We'll kick your ass from town to town."*

Bernie Taupin, eat your heart out. We even had a song called "The Ballad of Jeffery Dahmer," which was exactly as tactless and disgusting as you think it would be. Why didn't we make it big??

We spent our senior year rehearsing for what would be our first real gig at the Wreck Room in Atlanta. We were sure that we were going to blow the roof off the place. We had a stage, a drum riser, monitors, lights, everything. This was the real deal. We were the first of four bands and ended up playing to our parents, the other bands waiting to go on, and two guys who got into a scuffle back by the pool table. One of the bands who played with was Black Rabbit. Years later, one of the guys in the band named Andy would end up becoming a good friend of mine. He told me that it was their first gig as well and he remembered seeing us play and thinking, "Damn, if they can do it, we can do it." Not sure if that was an insult or a compliment!

After the gig, the door guy came up to us, gave us forty bucks, and said, "You kids are all right. You'll get better." Again, insult or compliment? We were kind of disappointed, but without a doubt, a seed had been planted. I had my first fix of performing live. I couldn't sleep a wink that night. I knew then that I wanted to do this for the rest of my life even if I didn't make any money. I also knew that things with Gutterslut needed to change. We had to get better, and I really wanted to play Heavy Metal music. But how would I manifest this vision?

Me on stage in my stonewashed jeans with
Rachael's Dead.
Atlanta, GA, 1993

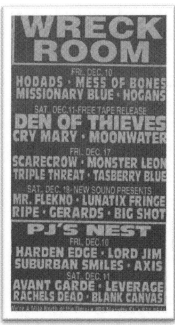

Our first time in *Creative Loafing*.
Yes, they spelled our name wrong.

Start Your Own Damn Band:
Part 2: Rachael's Dead

Soon reality set in, and we realized that if we wanted to go someplace with our music, Gutterslut needed to step it up. We unanimously agreed that we wanted to be a metal band. I didn't have the confidence to be a metal guitarist, so I decided I would play bass and we'd find a guitarist who could complete our vision. After jamming with a few people to no avail, we were introduced to a friend of a friend of a friend who supposedly was an awesome guitarist. He was a couple of years older than us, and honestly, he wasn't great, but he was way better than me, so he got the gig. And besides, he looked metal as fuck with his leather jacket and waist-length hair.

We were a band of merry men: a drummer who kept time like a clock with a dying battery, a guitarist who often soloed out of key, a decent singer, and a failed guitarist-turned-bassist. But we were an

127

honest-to-goodness metal band. We decided to put our punk roots and the Gutterslut name to rest and come up with a new band name. We started throwing around ideas. Midnight Knock. Sledgehammer. Narcolepsy. Perfect! Name our band after a medical condition in which a person just randomly falls asleep for no fucking reason. Then one night, I was listening to "Doin' the Nasty" by Slik Toxik. As the last song was playing, I picked up the CD case to read the song titles. The last song, an instrumental, was called "Rachel's Dead." I thought that name sounded awesome as fuck.

I brought it to the band, and they loved it. We changed the spelling to Rachael's Dead so Slik Toxik wouldn't sue us (like we thought we'd ever be big enough for them to know we existed). We also loved it because our singer's girlfriend's name was Rachel and we hated her more than split pea soup, so it was a win-win. Years later, I would become good friends with Slik Toxik guitarist Kevin Gale, and he told me that it was cool as fuck that we named our band after one of their songs. Note that he didn't offer his opinions on the music (insert laugh here).

People sometimes say that your band's first show is your best show. This definitely wasn't the case for Rachael's Dead. We played on, I think, a Thursday night, and my parents came along with maybe ten others. After our show, I asked my dad what he thought, and he said, "You guys are terrible, but you're better than Gutterslut. Besides, you were having the time of your life up there, and I'm sure you will get better. Just keep having fun." That was the most my dad had said to me in a long time, and that has stayed with me to this day. "Just keep having fun." That's what it's all about. You can be the best band in the world (a problem we would never have), but if you weren't having fun, what was the point?

We did get better. Not a ton better, but better. I mean, we didn't get amazing, but if we were at a 3 when we started, we were a solid 6.5 when I quit the band. Ok, maybe a 6. Either way, we played our asses off. We played every all-ages, metal dive club in Atlanta that we could: the Wreck Room, Somber Reptile, PJ's Nest, and we even played the prestigious and now-legendary Masquerade (on a Thursday night to twenty people). We played with bands like Rumblefish, Crawlspace, Smartass, Oliver Tricks, and Stuck Mojo, and we had a great time. We learned a lot by watching these bands, which we looked up to as seasoned professionals.

Some bands weren't so cool to play with. One in particular I remember was called 21 Down, a local band whose members probably changed your car's oil during the day but were pretentious fucks who acted like they were headlining an arena show. One night, we were opening for them at the Wreck Room, and after our set, I had to take a leak. At the old Wreck Room, the guy's bathroom was on the side of the stage. I was on my way to go to the bathroom, and some big guy, probably one of their friends, stopped me and said: "You'll have to wait because 21 Down is getting ready." I politely pushed past him and entered the restroom to take a leak while the guys from 21 Down primped in the mirrors for all thirty of their fans.

After this happened, I went back and told my band. Being the obnoxious kids that we were, we decided that we need to find a way to knock them off their high horses. They had these coasters that looked like records, and they had their own phone number on them (pre-website days, folks). I can't remember the number exactly, but let's just say that it was 555-DOWN. We each took a stack of coasters from the bar and with sharpies, changed the number to 555-DOODOO. We started handing them out around the room and tossed some up on the stage. "Who the fuck did this, man?" says the singer. We just laughed and left the venue. Damn, we were jerky kids.

We were significantly younger than the bands we were playing with, but they were totally cool going into "big brother" mode with me. While my singer was out fucking his girlfriend in the car and my drummer and guitarist were playing video games, I was hanging out with these guys who seemed to have their shit together, guys like Bones from Stuck Mojo and Rich from Oliver Tricks. I'd ask them about booking, about who to trust, who to not trust, how much money a band should make, etc. I would talk to the sound guy, the door guy, and even Toe, the owner of the Wreck Room, asking business questions and about the best ways to advertise shows. I was young, and I was soaking it all up like a sponge.

Taxi Haskell from Smartass was one of the coolest guys on the scene. He used to ruffle my hair whenever he'd see me and always have something positive to say. I was a huge fan of Smartass, so that was really cool. I remember running into Taxi at some amphitheater show. I can't remember which show, but I was chilling by myself sitting on a bench when he walked by and said, "Don!" I was shocked but stoked that he remembered me. We talked a little bit, and he told me, "Man, you know what I like about your band? You guys have heart, and you're not jaded… yet." We talked a bit longer, shook hands, and he walked off with some hot woman. There was some foreshadowing in that conversation.

For two years, Rachael's Dead would rehearse at Public Storage on Frontage Road in Forest Park, Georgia. Along with other Atlanta almost/could've/should've been legends like Lost Cauz, Asmodeus, and Fade to Winter (Hi, Chris & Beau), we all rehearsed our noisy art in preparation to play to our loyal fan base of about twelve people…maybe twenty-five if we were lucky on a Saturday night.

Sweating it out (or freezing our balls off) in that storage shed are some of my favorite memories. This is where my songwriting craft began to improve. It's where we started to grow as a band and where our drummer eventually learned to keep better time. Our songs got more complex in the arrangements, and my lyric writing started to take on a life of its own. We were heading someplace special, but like all good things, it had to end.

Our live shows were getting more attention, but I started to notice that I was drifting in a different direction from the other three guys in the band. I was discovering bands like Cathedral, Kyuss, and Crowbar, and I was really digging their sound. These bands pulled from other influences such as early Black Sabbath (which wasn't so common back then) and were presenting heavy music in a way that was new and refreshing to me. The other guys in the band were more excited about The Offspring and at one point, and even wanted to start covering one of their songs, "Self Esteem." I could feel a shift in the current, and I didn't like where it was taking me.

One Saturday night, we had the prime 9:00 p.m. slot at the Wreck Room and played to one of our biggest crowds. We closed our show out with a brand-new song that I had just written called "Personal Demons." It was an epic song that had dynamics, tempo changes, and even a very Iron Maiden-esque change in the middle where I did some bass chord playing that I stole from Iron Maiden's "Rime of the Ancient Mariner." It brought the house down, and I couldn't have been happier or felt more alive.

After our set, we were approached by a guy from another band who was bigger than ours (can't remember who to save my life) who

131

wanted us to make a trek down to Florida to open for them at some club. As much as I loved playing live, there was something that was holding me back from wanting to hit the road "on tour" (who I am kidding, it was one show in Florida). I knew the other guys in the band were going in a different direction musically and I was feeling outnumbered. But I couldn't express my emotions. Instead, I argued with the band that it wasn't smart to do the show in Florida. We had nothing in the form of merch, no demo tapes, no shirts, nothing. I said that we would lose money. The band just stared at me, dumbfounded. We packed up our shit in silence, and we all went home. I had a feeling something would be brewing after this exchange.

At our next rehearsal, I could tell I was walking into a shit storm. The guitarist looked at me and, without hesitation, said, "You are holding us back, and you're just negative. This isn't your band anymore." In retrospect, he was probably right, but it still hurt to hear. I packed my shit up, told them I'd come back the next day to get my gear, and in the biggest fuck you, my twenty-year-old self could muster, I left the band. They ended up getting another bassist, they did their Offspring covers, and much to my glee (come on, I was a bitter kid who had just left/been kicked out of his band), they got knocked back down to weeknights, and then they split up after a few more shows.

When I left the band, I put my bass in a closet, and I didn't play music for a while. I was frustrated, angry, and guess what? I was jaded, but I had learned a lot. I knew how to book gigs and how to promote a band. I learned that someone's word isn't usually worth shit unless it's signed on a dotted line, and most of all, I learned to stick to my guns. I learned to play and write from my heart and do what I truly want to do, not what will make me popular. As for Rachael's Dead, while we may not have been the best band, it was a stepping stone for a musical journey that would last for another two decades and counting.

In 2016, I reunited with my former bandmates. We congregated at the guitarist's house and caught up with each other. We shared twenty years of life stories and eventually ended up in the basement trying to remember some of our old songs. We sounded absolutely horrible, but we laughed. It was a lot of fun. And then we parted ways. I finally felt like I could close that chapter out with a smile. After all these years, that is something that not everyone gets to do.

The Grunge Takeover

When I was in high school, I noticed things were changing. The first thing? The change in the fashion of my classmates. The girls, who were usually all decked out in makeup and designer clothes, were wearing flannel shirts, ripped jeans, and Doc Martins. Soon I started hearing people talk about bands like Soundgarden, Pearl Jam, Nirvana, and Alice in Chains. Alice In Chains had been on my radar for a couple of years, but these other bands were new to my ears and delivered something different from my usual hard rock/metal norm.

Although I was still a metalhead at heart, some of the music I was listening to was starting to wear thin and lose its appeal, both lyrically and musically. This shift was kind of a welcome change. It was like the tide came in and washed away the Warrants and the Enuff Z' Nuffs and the LA Guns of the world to make way for a different sound. While I remember thinking it sounded new, looking back on it now, grunge music was really retro. It was retro before retro was retro.

I thought Soundgarden was absolutely fantastic. They had these Black Sabbath-inspired riffs with a singer who had a voice like it was given to him by a fucking Greek god or something. I mean, Chris Cornell could sing like it was nobody's business, and I loved it. *Badmotorfinger* was one of my favorite albums at the time, and *Louder Than Love* was a mainstay in my CD player for a long time.

Alice in Chains had *Facelift*, which was a fucking metal classic in its own right, but it was the release of *Dirt* that solidified them as an amazing force to be reckoned with. To me, Alice in Chains was the seedy underbelly of humanity in raw, heavy music form. I mean, shit, you had a frontman up there singing songs to the masses that were open about his drug addiction. They had songs about being completely obliterated and knocked down by heroin, and then songs about the struggles of trying to kick it. This was a far cry from *"She's my cherry pie."* This was some heavy shit.

Pearl Jam scratched an itch I never knew I had. They looked like a rock band, dirty and raw, and they could play like motherfuckers. Mike McCready and Stone Gossard were (and still are) easily one of the best guitar duos in the biz. These guys played off each other like they were telepathic. It was kind of "jammy" before the jam band scene came around. Their sound was reminiscent of Crazy Horse if they actually played with dynamics and tuned their fucking guitars. They also had a lead singer who sounded like no other I had ever heard. I'm sure Eddie Vedder would kick my ass or cry or some shit if I called him a rock star, but fuck it. Vedder was a monster frontman who was a cross between

Roger Daltrey and Jim Morrison, making him a fucking rock star whether he liked that word or not.

Pearl Jam's music was refreshing, and I needed to find out where their sound originated. I was sure that the guys had to have been in other bands, so I started to dig. Through reading interviews and watching MTV (we still didn't have the internet in our homes), I learned some interesting shit. First, I found out that they had originally called themselves Mookie Blaylock after some basketball player. And that they came together after the demise of a band called Mother Love Bone, which had featured Pearl Jam members Jeff Ament (bassist) and Gossard. I immediately went to the local Record Bar and managed to pick up one of the last pieces of vinyl in the store, which happened to be the Mother Love Bone album *Apple*. At this point, CDs were starting to dominate the world as *the* music medium, so looking back, to get this on vinyl was a great find. I took that album home and put it on, and it changed my life forever.

Mother Love Bone was heavy when they needed to be, but they had this groove that I had never heard before. When I heard Mother Love Bone, Pearl Jam suddenly made sense to me. Not long after buying *Apple,* a friend of mine gave me a cassette of the band's *Shine* EP. The lyrics were eclectic, smart, cheeky, and sometimes dark. If you've ever heard a singer who sings a song that makes you feel like you're looking into the deepest, darkest corner of their soul, then you know what I'm talking about when I say Mother Love Bone's music was something magical. "This is Shangri-La" was a song I could relate to because of my love for performing live music. "Bone China" and its haunting lyrics, the happy, hippie melodic tones of "Come Bite the Apple," and the heavy groove of "Stardog Champion" hooked me in. To this day, "Man of Golden Words" makes me wish that the world would see and hear music the way Andrew did.

While some great bands were ushered in with this new era, there were still a lot of shitty ones. I know Nirvana was huge, and Kurt Cobain was the icon to many, but honestly, I feel bad that those kids had such a shitty guitarist, singer, and songwriter as their icon. Was it Cobain himself as an artist, or was it his ideals and attitude that put him on that pedestal? Hell, if I would've been those kids, I think I would've been happier having Chris Cornell or Andrew Wood as the spokesperson of my generation. Then again, I'm an old curmudgeon, so what do I know?

The "grunge" era, in my opinion, wasn't so much as an invasion as it was cleaning house. Suddenly, not having an image was the new image. Bands like RATT, Warrant, and Poison, who once dominated MTV, were sent packing, not to be seen or heard from again until years later as nostalgia pieces, which honestly worked out for them. The movement made way for music rather than an image to become the focus, whether it was great bands like Alice Chains and Soundgarden or terrible ones like Nirvana and Mudhoney. It was a new form of expression, and if anything, it was a wakeup call to bands all over that they couldn't just dial it in and play it safe. Maybe it lit a fire under the asses of many musicians to strive for something better.

Me, Art, Richard Cole & Edan Everly Walk Into Restroom

Everyone has one of those stories. You know the one I'm talking about. The kind of story that when someone starts telling it, a group of people surround the storyteller like a donut, eyes wide open, ears open, with a look of attentiveness. This is one of those stories.

Back in 1992, while living in Atlanta, a couple of friends and I decided at the last minute to see a Van Nuys, California-based band called Rhino Bucket that sounded eerily like Bon Scott-era AC/DC. They were one of our favorite bands, but we had never seen them live. They were touring for their second album, *Get Used to It*, and playing at the local club, the Masquerade. If I recall, it was a Saturday night, and it was like one-tenth full, maybe only about 60-70 people.

The opening band was called Edan. After getting a free sampler a few weeks before the show, I picked up their album *Dead Flowers*.

139

They had this Black Crowes/Quireboys barroom rock thing going on, which at the time was very popular. I really enjoyed the album and was looking forward to seeing them live. Before their set, I headed to the bathroom to take a leak. I'm just standing there at a urinal, and all of a sudden, this guy walks in and starts pissing next to me. I look over, and it's my buddy Art Howard from one of my favorite Atlanta bands, Zen. We get done pissing, and we're just hanging out in the bathroom talking when all of a sudden this guy walks in and introduces himself to us as Edan.

It didn't take a brain surgeon to figure out that by his name, stage clothes, and amazing hair that this dude was the singer of the band Edan, which obviously is named after him. So now there are three guys just hanging out in the restroom just shooting the shit. Art and I were asking Edan about being on the road, being signed to a real record deal, etc. when suddenly a very big and kind of scary Englishman comes bursting into the bathroom shouting, "Where's my fucking lead singer?" Art and I look at the guy with looks of shock and awe as Edan says, "Richard, meet my new friends Don and Art." It turns out that the band's manager is none other than Richard Cole. Art and I looked at each other in disbelief and said, "*The* Richard Cole? As in the Led Zeppelin tour manager, Richard Cole?" Richard Cole says, "It's a pleasure to meet you, chaps." We look at him, dumbfounded, and shook his hand. We end up talking for a few minutes, and then Richard Cole says, "Nice to meet you, fellas, but we have a fucking show to do." And with that, they exited the bathroom, leaving Art and me just standing there laughing. Who would ever believe this?

I made my way back out to the front of the stage, told my friends what just happened, and watched Edan play a solid 45-

minute opening set, which we really dug. To make the story even better, at the end of the show, we find out that Edan's full name is Edan Everly, as in son of Don Everly of the legendary Everly Brothers and kid brother to Erin Everly who, by that time, was the ex-Mrs. Axl Rose. And just when you thought it couldn't get any weirder, the drummer was the son of Frankie Avalon, the teen heartthrob, the Beach Blanket Bingo pimp himself who I'm sure had his hand up Annette Funicello's shirt many a time.

After all of this excitement, one would think that watching Rhino Bucket would seem like small potatoes in comparison, but when Rhino Bucket took the stage opening with "One Night Stand," they proceeded to kick my ass for nearly two hours of sweaty, sleazy, loud rock & roll. It was hands down one of the greatest live club shows I have ever seen, and I still talk about how fucking great that band was live. After the show, we even hung out with their singer/guitarist Georg Dolivo, who was super fucking cool and took plenty of time with us to talk about music, sign our shit, and take photos.

After all these years, this story still follows me and continues to be a great table story at lunch with friends old and new.

1992: Iron Maiden plays a sold-out show
in a 19,000 seat amphitheater

1996: Iron Maiden plays to a half full, 1,100 seat club
(ticket stub courtesy of my best friend James)

Not Going Down with the Ship

The mid-'90s was a grim time for hard rock and metal bands. Many of the bands who were once cool were now laughing stocks to the flannel-clad, baggy shorts, chain-wallet-wearing kids. The bands seemed tired and worn out, and it felt like some of them just couldn't compete with the changing musical climate. Bruce Dickinson leaving Iron Maiden, Rob Halford exiting Judas Priest to make techno/industrial music, and Dave Mustaine wearing flannel were signs of just where metal was heading. Metallica cut off their hair. Things were starting to look grim for metal.

To be fair, there were some new hard rock/metal bands putting out quality music like the roots-rock sounds of Tora Tora, the unique technical/sleaze metal of Slik Toxik, and even Cathedral, who were one of the forefathers of the modern doom/Sabbath Worship genre. But they didn't seem to stand a chance at achieving the commercial success of those that came before them by just a few years. They were outnumbered 20:1, and most, if not all, of these bands, barely made it past the sophomore album phase. This was disappointing because I think some of these bands, if given a chance, could've done some great shit, but they were too late to the party.

The end was coming, and it wasn't graceful. It was more like bursting into flames as all the Heavy Metal souls cried out in terror and were suddenly silenced. Yeah, I stole that line and bonus points if you know where I stole it from. To be clear, things weren't looking good for metal. Bands like Korn, Limp Bizkit, Disturbed, and Machine Head were moving in, and to be honest, I didn't connect with them, and I sure as hell didn't like them.

In my youth, Twisted Sister and Dio were there for me when I felt like I needed to be understood. Listening to their music would almost put me at ease; they could make me not so mad at the world. But this new generation of metal seemed to do the opposite, channeling the anger in young suburbanites to dangerous ends. Instead of giving kids a positive relief or outlook on society, these new bands were encouraging fans to lash out, break stuff, and smash shit up.

As an adult, I found it ridiculous. For some reason, it almost seemed anti-metal to me. There was just no way I could see myself getting on board with this crap. Suddenly, I felt like that old guy watching bands playing their down-tuned guitars and singing their shitty, angsty lyrics... GET OF MY FUCKING LAWN ALREADY!

Eventually, the bands that did manage to hang on started making shitty records and trying to change a bit with the climate, which made things even worse. Iron Maiden, Megadeth, and even Judas Priest were putting out some of the worst material of their

144

careers. They started playing smaller venues. In Atlanta, Iron Maiden and Judas Priest went from packing arenas to playing the Masquerade, the same club that my band Rachael's Dead played at and KISS was playing to less than half full arenas. I don't know if they were attempting to try and stay afloat in the ocean, but their ships were sinking. It was a truly sad time for me, and I was convinced that metal was done for good.

I consoled myself with the fact that I still had the classics. I would always have *Live After Death*, *Defenders of the Faith*, *Master of Puppets*, and *Rust in Peace*. I remember thinking, "Man, it was a good run." Fifteen years or so for a lot of these bands meant they left behind a legacy of music vast enough to last us all for the rest of our lives.

Ok, I'm being a little dramatic, it's not like it all came and went in a flash of the blade. I had no clue that Bruce Dickinson was still making amazing albums, which I discovered many years later thanks to my best friend, James. While metal seemed to have a fork stuck in it, I always knew that the music that was there for me as a kid all those years ago would still be there for me as an adult. I also remember thinking to myself that all things seem to work in cycles. Music is a very cyclical thing; it's forever changing yet revolving at the same time. While it took a lot longer than I expected, the classic metal that I grew up with and loved eventually did make its way back around.

Backstage and ready to rock with my roots/rock
band Collins Drive.
Atlanta, GA, 2020

Being Un-Metal

I consider myself a metalhead, and I've been one for well over thirty years. But I also have zero problems admitting that I like probably some of the most un-metal shit. I had the same three or four friends from 10th–12th grade, and we were a really open-minded group of kids. We saw absolutely no problem liking Poison, Tangier, or even Winger, yet at the same time loving Suicidal Tendencies, Queensryche, Black Sabbath, Megadeth, and Venom. Hell, we even appreciated and loved The Allman Brothers Band, The Animals, Jellyfish, The Ramones, and I've been a diehard fan of the Monkees since 1985. In my opinion, that is fucking metal.

Why is that metal? Isn't the point of being a metalhead not to give a flying fuck what anybody thinks? Being a metalhead means standing by your bands and never hiding your love for the music that moves you and makes you feel fucking good. So couldn't being metal also mean taking that mentality across the board, no matter what genre you like?

I think it is way more fucking metal for Tom Hunting, drummer for thrash legends Exodus, to express his love for Journey than it is for Phil Anselmo to tell you to "walk on home, boy." Remember Winger? People considered them the most un-metal band you could be. When I interviewed Kip Winger, he told me, "Metallica had some good stuff in the old days, but now they're just musically bankrupt." Man, if that's not metal...I don't know what is!

I believe that metalheads are some of the most open-minded, wholehearted, passionate people I know. I personally know metalheads who will tell you just how much they fucking love Behemoth but then turn around and talk about their favorite classical composer. I know metalheads who will listen to the doomiest of doom metal but then rave about the best jazz music they heard while in New Orleans. Hell, I know someone who runs a metal blog and plays guitar and sings in a roots/rock band (that would be me). I don't know about you, but I'd consider these people to be the most metal of them all.

Being un-metal is, without a doubt, the most metal thing you can do. Period. It isn't a sign of weakness or vulnerability, but a sign of a true, honest, and cultured person who stands by the most un-metal music that they love with conviction, honor, and passion. To be unapologetic about the non-metal things you love and to express it to people with honesty is the most metal thing you can do.

So metalheads, go listen to John Coltrane. Enjoy *Open Up and Say Ah* by Poison. Get your groove on to some Jamiroquai and spark up to some Grateful Dead because being metal isn't about simply listening to metal and nothing else. Being metal is about being an individual, being yourself, and saying "fuck you" to anyone who wants to shit on you for it. It's also about engaging with naysayers and others to try and turn them on to aspects of metal music that they may enjoy. As I am writing this, I'm listening to Poison's *Flesh and Blood* album, and I'm enjoying the living fuck out of this while wearing a Venom shirt. Then I'm going to rehearse with my roots/rock band. Metal as fuck!

It's not every day you get to have hummus with a
legend. Me & Bruce Dickinson.
Atlanta, GA, 1993

Me, Bruce Dickinson, and Hummus

Back in 1994, I managed to maintain the same non-cool status I had in high school. I know, crazy, right? I was twenty years old, still living at home, single, hanging out with the same three friends from high school, and working as an assistant manager for some shitty fast food restaurant called Gyro Wrap at the local mall. Wow, typing that alone made me want to fucking drink, but in all honesty, I wouldn't change a damn thing. Why? Because no matter how miserable I was, I had music. And the music always got me through.

Regardless of how shitty my life seemed at the time, I sure did manage to have a lot of really cool experiences that made being me not such a bad thing. Matter of fact, my whole life has been a long series of serendipitous experiences, things that most people would never believe unless someone was there to see it or I had a camera to capture the moment. One particular instance took place on July 5, 1994, in Atlanta, GA.

So there I am, working this crap fast food gig in the mall as a short-order cook in a food court joint that reeked of meat, onions, and grease. There were days I would pull twelve-hour shifts and wish for a fucking meteor to land on the mall or for some other catastrophic disaster that would get me the hell out of there. One of the things I used to love to do to escape was to go to the record stores (CD stores at this point) in the mall and shoot the shit with the people who worked there. At those two stores, I managed to become friends with two really cool people: Chris, who worked at Record Bar, and Donna at Camelot Music. I envied their awesome jobs. I would frequently hang out in the stores to talk music with them, and they were always cool, hooking me up with posters, free promos, etc.

One day, when I managed to get a day off, I was sitting in my room alone, listening to music on my headphones and going wherever the music took me. My phone rang (I had my own phone line. How adult of me!), breaking me out of my musical trance, and it was Donna from Camelot Music. Donna called me up and said, "Don. I know you're a huge Iron Maiden fan. I have some trivia questions for you." Confused yet intrigued at the same time, I played along. She asked me, "Who was the original singer for Iron Maiden?" "Too Easy! Paul Day." She said, "Wow, ok, I thought it was Paul Di'Anno." "What is the first album Bruce Dickinson sang on?" "Again, too easy. *Number of the Beast*." "Ok, finally, what is the name of Iron Maiden's mascot?" "Really, Donna? It's Eddie."

"I'm very impressed, Don," she said. "Final question: Who would like to attend the invitation-only album release party for Bruce Dickinson's upcoming solo album?" I was in shock, and I made her

152

repeat the question. Laughing, she said, "Don, I can't think of anyone who would appreciate this more than you. Come get this invitation." I was ecstatic, so I made my way over to Camelot Music to pick up the invite. When I got there, Donna looked at me laughing and said, "You look like you're about to explode with excitement!" Well, that's because I was.

When I look back, I am reminded that this was a very awkward time for not just me, but metal in general. The winds of change were upon us, and things were looking weird. Metal bands were cutting their hair, Megadeth was wearing flannel, and Bruce Dickinson had quit Iron Maiden. Additionally, I had walked away from my metal band in part because they wanted to start covering Offspring songs. So, you can imagine my feeling of loss and confusion. All I knew was that through all this, I was about to meet Bruce Dickinson. I called my buddy Phil and asked if he'd be my guest, and he was nearly as fucking psyched as I was.

The night of the event, we gathered our *Tattooed Millionaire* albums and Maiden picture discs, stopped off at Eckerd's to pick up a couple of Sharpies for autographs, and made our way to the venue. As always, we arrived about an hour early, and right away, we learned that this wasn't going to be like the shows we were used to attending. We figured we'd get there early to get a good place and all that shit, but when we got there, it was just us. We killed time by sitting out in front of the venue, smoking cigarettes and pacing around in nervous excitement. We had never been to this venue. It was a new place called Smith's Olde Bar (formerly Gene & Gabes).

As we approached the door to go in, security stopped us, looked at our Iron Maiden shirts, and said, "You guys don't look like you're supposed to be here." Uh, how could that be? We have Iron

Maiden shirts on! Before he could turn us away, I showed him my invitation, and he looked at me in shock and said, "Wow. Ok, you *are* official. Have a good time." When we got inside, we were shocked. There were already several people inside. We looked around and noticed that the place was full of people in "work casual" attire and suits. Wow. What was this? We scouted out the situation, and there were tables. Wow, so fancy. We found a table with a great view near the side of the stage, and we made our way there and took our seats.

First, we were treated to a premiere of Bruce's new video for the song "Tears of the Dragon." I remember feeling completely blown away and getting goosebumps from the sheer awesomeness of the song and the video. It sounded so different from Maiden, but it sounded like Bruce was making a change for himself, and I loved where it was going. Soon after the video was done, the curtain opened, and there was Bruce and guitarist Alex Dickson on stage with acoustic guitars. Bruce and Alex did a great acoustic set that featured brand new songs such as "Hell No," "Cyclops," and "Tears of the Dragon." There were a few more songs in there, but I was too busy getting my face blown off to remember to write down any kind of setlist. It was a fantastic performance, and then soon after, Bruce was making his way through the crowd.

My buddy and I, trying to be as cool as possible, decided we'd let Bruce do his thing, and we'd eventually get our moment with him. To kill time, we made our way over to the buffet. We got ourselves a free beer (weren't even carded!), and we scoped out the food. This place was decked out. There was a buffet spread of some weird fucking food that we had no idea what it was. We recognized the carrots and fruit, but there were pita bread wedges and this kind of weird-looking spread that smelled like nothing I had ever smelled.

We got some anyway and went back to our table. We nursed our free Rolling Rocks, took photos of each other clowning around, and suddenly, there he was, the man himself approaching our table.

Bruce walked up to us, smiled, and said, "You guys don't look like you're supposed to be here. I like that. May I join you?" Bruce pulled up a seat, and right away, we told him how much we liked the new tunes. He was so cool and calm and told us how excited he was for the new album.

Then, the question of the night was asked. My buddy says, "Bruce, can I ask you a question?" Bruce said, "Of course. What is it?" My buddy then points to his plate and says, "Bruce, what the fuck is this?" Bruce let out a huge laugh and said, "That's hummus and pita bread, my friend." as he laughed some more. He thanked us for coming out, graciously signed our stuff, and took photos with us (even after singing "Cyclops," which is about how cameras steal your soul). He then said, "You guys really made my night. Thank you for being here!" and with that, he was gone into the crowd.

I will never forget July 5, 1994, and recounting it here took me back. It's moments like this that make me smile and say, "You know what? It's good to be me." Meeting Bruce Dickinson was something I never thought would even be remotely possible, much less sitting at a table with him drinking free Rolling Rocks and eating hummus and pita bread. By the way, the hummus was fucking disgusting.

What a long strange trip, indeed. Me & my wife
Lizzi at the Grateful Dead Fare Thee Well Tour.
Chicago, IL, 2015

What a Long, Strange Trip: From Metalhead to Folk Singing Deadhead

After quitting Rachael's Dead in 1994, in a young and very stupid manner, I pretty much destroyed everything I had related to the band. I burned my lyrics, nearly all the photos, and just about anything else. I was ready to just be *done*, to write them off. I then auditioned for a few metal bands that played more along the lines of newer metal bands. "Do you down-tune, dude?" "Do you play five-string bass?" "Do you like to play sludge?" I decided that it was a fine time for me to take a break from it all. I put my bass, bass cabinet, and head in the closet, closed it, and didn't think twice.

I had a feeling that I would be called back to music, but I didn't know how or when. I found myself on a quest for something new. I wanted an escape from all the volume, the feedback, the distorted guitars, the drunk and disorderly, etc. I wanted a new scene. I found myself deep in my father's folk music collection. It was the polar opposite of metal, but there was a heaviness to the songs lyrically and emotionally. Crosby, Stills, Nash, Joan Baez, Buffy Sainte Marie, Carole King, Donovan, Bob Dylan, you name it. If it was folkie kind of shit, he had it.

I really enjoyed this music. "Suite: Judy Blue Eyes"? "Codine"? "So Far Away"? Are you fucking kidding me? These songs were so mellow yet so heavy that they penetrated my soul. I wanted more. One day, MTV was on in the background and I happened to see the video for the song "What Would You Say" by Dave Matthews Band. For some reason, Dave Matthews Band hit me like a ton of bricks. It was so different from anything I had ever heard. I was hooked.

Dave Matthews Band woke something inside of me, and I was in love with music again. Like the music junkie I am, I wanted more. I started to hear from other fans of Dave Matthews Band about Blues Traveler, the Spin Doctors (who I already knew of), and this little band from Georgia called Allgood. I felt like I was discovering music for the first time all over again. The rest of 1994 and into the summer of 1995 was spent immersing myself in these bands. But I had yet to latch onto the big kahunas of the scene.

In 1995, I took a part-time job waiting tables at a bar and grill in Jonesboro called Winstons. I think it's a closed dry cleaner now. I took the job to make some extra money and to fill in the time my band used to fill. One slow weeknight, I was waiting on this guy at the bar, and he asked if I was into the Grateful Dead. "Nah, I'm not into all that acid shit," I told him. "Man, you'd be surprised if you really gave them a chance." He then asked me if I liked Phish. I had never even heard of them, but he told me the next time he was in, he would bring me a mixtape.

A week later, here comes dude with a mixtape of his favorite Phish songs. My first impression was, "These lyrics are absolutely

158

insane." My second impression was, "These motherfuckers can play their asses off." He told me about tape trading (where fans trade bootlegged copies of live shows), but it was so beyond me that I didn't get it. He told me to go out and buy *A Live One* by Phish. I bought it, and I was blown away. Then I bought *Junta*, then *Lawn Boy*, then *Rift*, then *A Picture of Nectar*, then *Hoist*, and suddenly, I was a full-blown Phish head.

Phish revved me up and got me excited. Maybe it was because they were so off the wall. Maybe it was the musicianship. Maybe it was that it wasn't Limp Bizkit and Korn or whatever the fuck was taking over metal. Then I did what just about everyone my age was doing: I bought a computer. An Acer 166 Pentium with a 56K modem—at the time, one of the fastest computers on the market. I took the monstrosity home, got an AOL account, and checked out a chat room called the Phish Bowl. It was like going through the wardrobe into Narnia.

It was here that I learned the art of tape trading and immediately became a full-on bootleg tape trader. I started to get turned on to other amazing bands like God Street Wine, Strangefolk, The Recipe, Acoustic Junction, and countless others. This was also where hearing the Grateful Dead would spark a fire that burns bright to this very day.

This guy (I wish I could remember his name so I could thank him) who I was trading tapes with asked me one day in a private chat if I liked the Grateful Dead. "There's no Dead on your tape list. Why is this?" I told him it was because I thought they were just kind of noisy and that I didn't like all of that spacey shit. He told me, "Let me make you a mix, and I promise it will change your life." First, he advised me, "Go buy *Skeletons from the Closet*. It's a 'best of' compilation that will show you that the Dead actually had some great songs. I bought the CD, and I was amazed at what I was hearing. Then his tape arrived. "Box of Rain," "Morning Dew (Live)," "Help on the Way > Slipknot > Franklin's Tower," "Dire Wolf," and so much more. The minute I heard "Box of Rain," I cried like a fucking baby. It was so beautiful, and I was on my way to becoming a lifelong Deadhead.

I'm not religious, but listening to the Grateful Dead was a spiritual experience for me. I had never heard anything like it. The lyrics and the music moved me, making me cry and laugh. It also made me want to express my emotions to others through music. Not even a week later, I was at the local music store, Atina's, buying a Takamine acoustic guitar. I took it home and immediately I started playing it. I started writing lyrics and music. No, they weren't very good, but that fire was rekindled, and I felt like I had nothing to slow me down. I had no limitations, nobody to tell me what would and what wouldn't work. It was such a cathartic feeling to fall in love with making music again. No, I never lost my love for Heavy Metal. I still listened to my Iron Maiden, Judas Priest, KISS, Metallica, and others, but I had found a style of music that made me feel like I could be myself and express myself better than I ever could as a Metal musician.

On March 26, 27, 29, and 30 of 1995, the Grateful Dead were performing their annual multi-night run at the Omni in Atlanta. An old friend of mine had an extra ticket to see them on March 30th and asked me if I wanted to go. "Man, I'd love to go, but I have to work. I'll catch them next year." I had no idea that the opportunity would never come back around because, on August 9th of 1995, Jerry Garcia passed away. I was devastated. It was the first time besides the day

Cliff Burton of Metallica died where I truly felt the impact of losing a musician who meant so much to so many people. I was in New Orleans with my parents, visiting my uncle. We were listening to Edie Brickell and the New Bohemians on the stereo when the news on TV announced that Jerry Garcia was dead. I remember my mom just looking over at me and saying, "I'm sorry, Donald." Even that early on, she knew how much of an impact the Dead made on me in such a short time.

From that moment, it was my mission to be a singer/songwriter. For the next twenty-plus years, I would write countless songs, play numerous shows, and release solo acoustic albums. I performed in three bands and, with my current band, Collins Drive. I continue to make music, and I don't see stopping in the foreseeable future. I never forget the impact of the Grateful Dead, Dave Matthews Band, Phish, and many others. Even though I would eventually find myself growing out of some of these groups, the one that never seemed to be lost on me was the Grateful Dead. If anything, the older I got and the longer that I was a musician, the more important their music became to me.

Over the years, I have seen every post-Grateful Dead-related project. It has been my mission never to pass up an opportunity to see these amazing, touching, and soul-crushing songs performed by surviving members of the band. These days, Bob Weir, Mickey Hart, and Billy Kruetzman are touring with John Mayer, Oteil Burbridge, and Jeff Chimenti as Dead & Company. It has easily been the best representation of the Dead's legacy since Jerry left us and the music continues to move me, inspire me, and make me happy to be alive.

While most Metal shows have a parking scene full of black shirts, tailgating, and beer-chugging, The Deadhead scene is unlike anything you could ever imagine. It's an ocean of tie-dyed shirts, floppy hats, and some of the biggest smiles you'll ever see. It's a traveling circus of freaks that transform simple, gravel parking lots into a counter-cultural outside mall, also known as Shakedown Street. On Shakedown Street, you can find anything and everything—grilled cheese sandwiches, cold beer, shirts, jewelry, and a variety of "party favors" that will enhance the live music experience. Most of all, you meet some of the kindest, most giving, and loving people. Strangers hugging and dancing together while music fills the air. This is my bliss and my "happy place."

Being a Deadhead, hippie, peace-loving freak, I can still love my metal and always have an undying connection and love for the music that changed my life forever. But it's also nice to know that there was a whole other soundtrack for a different chapter of my life. They are two very different chapters but both huge parts of the story that made me the person I am today.

The Internet: The Best Thing to Happen to Metal Dorks

In my youth, I spent countless hours sitting in my room listening to what the fuck ever and reading (and even re-reading) my stacks of Metal magazines. *Circus*, *Hit Parader*, *Metal Edge*, *Faces Rocks*, *RIP Magazine*, you name it, I had it. In the back of *Hit Parader* and *Circus* magazines, there were advertisements for catalogs that offered bootlegs, 8x10s of my heroes in action on stage, and t-shirts. I would send off a self-addressed stamped envelope (SASE for you youngins) and check the mail daily until the catalog arrived. Once it did, I would spend hours studying it carefully page by page. I was in heaven.

KISS bootlegs, Mötley Crüe bootlegs, Iron Maiden bootlegs, they had it all. Most were available on cassette, others on vinyl, with crazy-ass artwork. I would circle the ones I wanted with a fine-tip-pen knowing damn good and well I would never be able to get them.

Why? The prices were usually astronomical. Actually, they were probably like $25 or so, but when you're eleven years old, $25 is like six months' salary. I remember the holy grail for me was when I had heard about a "full version" of Iron Maiden's *Maiden Japan* live EP. The commercial release only had four songs on it, but this was the full show, baby, the full kit and caboodle with a drum solo and everything. I had to have this one, but it wasn't meant to be.

As years went by and I got older, I started going to record shows. These record shows were like huge-ass dork conventions. People who were collectors of music of all kinds would flock to these places to buy, sell, and trade some of the most useless shit ever known to man, but for people like me, it was like unearthing a hotel ballroom full of holy grails.

In the metal world, there are quite a few of these holy grails. That Iron Maiden show I mentioned earlier, *Bats Head Soup* by Ozzy Osbourne, which is an LP made from the original tapes that would later become the *Tribute* album, Ozzy Osbourne's *Mr. Crowley* picture disc that contained an unreleased song called "You Said It All", and Mötley Crüe's original Leathur Records release of their debut, *Too Fast For Love*, just to name a few. The only problem is that much like everything else, as time passes, the costs and demand for these items increase.

What I had the opportunity to get ten years prior for like twenty bucks was now $50 or $60. The issue was that at this time, I was a fast-food cook making eight bucks an hour, so needless to say, this wasn't going to happen. I would occasionally save lots of money over the course of a year so that when the record show would come around, I'd have the dough to pick up something cool like that long sought after Mötley Crüe bootleg from Fresno in '85 or, even better, the two-record set of Mötley Crüe from the *Girls Girls Girls* tour in Seattle. And maybe add to that a bootleg VHS tape of Twisted Sister on the *Come Out & Play* tour which was super rare. Those three items would probably set me back about a total of $125 or so.

Finding these items was a conquest. I was on a mission, and the thrill of the hunt was (and still is) fucking addictive. Once found and obtained, like a knight of King Arthur's Court, I proudly collected my findings and took them home to their proper resting place. Once home, I would play them, carefully put them into plastic sleeves, and proudly display them on my wall, hoping to make my friends completely jealous that they didn't have them.

Let's fast forward many years to about 2005 or so. The internet started to become a virtual "record show" for me, a place for me to find things that, as an eleven-year-old dork, I could only dream of getting my hands on. Peer-to-peer file sharing, BitTorrents, and blogs started popping up all over the internet full of live bootleg downloads of not only all the shows I ever wanted as a kid but tons more I never knew ever existed.

Remember that Iron Maiden show I mentioned? That was the very first bootleg I downloaded from the internet. I found it on some bootleg blog, and I couldn't wait to download it, artwork and everything. I downloaded it, played it, and let me tell you that it was worth every fucking year I waited to hear this thing. As a grown man, I felt all the excitement that I probably would've felt as a kid, but for some reason, it felt better. The clarity, the crispness, the professional quality of the sound just made it worth all those years of doing without it. I still listen to it to this day with the same level of enthusiasm and happiness.

So back to the hunt I went. What else would I find? Soon it would be live DVDs of Black Sabbath in Paris in 1970, Led Zeppelin demos and rarities, recordings of Bon Scott's pre-AC/DC band Fraternity, Dio live bootlegs from the *Holy Diver* and *Last In Line* tours on both audio and video. It was almost as if I had been let loose into one those bootleg catalogs on a limitless shopping spree that cost me all of nothing. All of these gems were made possible by a file-sharing program called Napster. Little would I know that this would be a program that many would blame for the fall of the music industry due to users illegally sharing music with others without pay. As for me, I was just there for the bootlegs.

Some may say that the magic of the hunt is gone with the introduction of file sharing on the internet for things like this, but the countless blogs, file-sharing programs, and bit torrent sites have made so many of my wishes come true. It's like being an archaeologist unearthing treasures that have been rumored to exist. At one time, I could only read and view these holy grails of music, but now I can possess them. I can enjoy them in all their glory.

What Comes Around, Goes Around

I remember listening to bands like Iron Maiden, Judas Priest, Metallica, and Anthrax—among countless others— and hearing my father say stuff like, "Those guys won't be here twenty years from now." I tried arguing that his folks said the same of The Beatles and Elvis Presley, and his only response was, "They made good songs. These bands are just loud and obnoxious." But Heavy Metal is like a weed of sorts or maybe even cockroaches in the sense that it is impossible to kill. Just when you think it's gone, here it comes again. It may look and sound slightly different, but it'll grow just as tall and fast as it did before.

In 2010, I was made aware of a band out of California called White Wizzard. They were a band with an old-school Heavy Metal "fuck you" attitude. Their sound was both energetic and melodic with twin guitar harmonies and well-constructed songs delivered by a vocalist named Wyatt Anderson, who sounded like he could crush a human skull in a single scream. They channeled the classic metal sound of old and lived up to the title of their album *Over the Top,* pushing the envelope of what was cool. Founding member and bassist/songwriter Jon Leon said that one of the reasons he formed White Wizzard was because he was tired of hearing this "Nu Metal" genre of down-tuned guitars with recordings saturated by Auto-Tune and backing tapes.

After I discovered White Wizzard, I fell deep into a rabbit hole of NWOTHM: New Wave of Traditional Heavy Metal. For those of you who aren't familiar, NWOTHM is the modern version of the New Wave of British Heavy Metal movement (NWOBHM). The NWOBHM featured bands like Iron Maiden, Saxon, Motorhead, Grim Reaper, Angel Witch, Judas Priest, and Diamond Head that offered an alternative to the rising punk movement of the 1980s. The more recent NWOTHM is playing a similar role in offering an alternative to the modern metal bands reigning arenas like Avenged Sevenfold, Five Finger Death Punch, and Rob Zombie. It would be damn near impossible to name all of the great NWOTHM bands, but bands such as 3 Inches of Blood, Holy Grail, Vindicator, Enforcer, Widow, Striker, Savage Master, and Christian Mistress are just the tip of the iceberg.

For an old dude like me, it was exciting to see young people rising up and forming bands in the vein of the elders. Going to shows was fun again. Being up front against the stage in a tiny, dank, dive bar headbanging and thrusting my fists in the air took me back to the days when that's what it was all about (who am I kidding, I last about ten minutes at the front before moving to the barstool at the back of the bar). The music is loud, the songs are well-constructed, melodic, and most of the bands make an effort to put on a high-energy show. In a nutshell, it is nice to see that the metal I knew and loved so much wasn't dead but alive, well, and thriving in the underground, again, just like it's forefathers once did.

It's also really comforting to know that there is a whole new generation of bands keeping that classic sound alive today. Will they ever be as big as Iron Maiden or Judas Priest? I wish I could say that they will be, but honestly, I doubt it. The times have changed so drastically. I believe that with the internet and home recording, the metal scene (and other scenes) has become oversaturated. Had bands like Holy Grail, Sabaton, and 3 Inches of Blood been around in the '80s, there's a good chance they would playing arenas at this point. These bands are also releasing stellar albums and putting on arena-level live shows in dive bars to small but dedicated followings.

I've had the pleasure of interviewing NWOTHM bands such as Striker, Savage Master, and Holy Grail, and they all express a hardcore dedication to classic Heavy Metal. They are grounded and realize that the reality is that they may never become arena bands. They understand that playing the music that they love to small audiences is what maintains the pulse on a genre of metal that many people in the mainstream metal scene considered dead.

What was old is now new. A whole new generation has the opportunity to experience classic metal in a second wave that will hopefully point them in the direction of what we grew up with. Not only has this music lasted for well over thirty-five years, but it has created an offspring that will hopefully last another twenty years to carry the torch when the elders are gone.

After a night of dancing madly backwards, I
had the honor of hanging out with legendary
Captain Beyond drummer Bobby Caldwell.
Atlanta, GA, 2017

Hey Man, Have you Heard Captain Beyond?

"Hey man, have you ever heard Captain Beyond?" If you've ever listened to Captain Beyond, you probably heard this very question from some buddy of yours before you did. Am I right? I mean, when did you ever hear a Captain Beyond song on the radio? And no, Sirius XM radio doesn't count! Yeah, that's what I thought. Just turn on the radio right now, and I'll bet that you'll hear Led Zeppelin, Boston, some shitty George Thoroughgood song, and maybe, if you're lucky, you'll get some sweet-ass deep cut from Jethro Tull. Ok, more than likely it'll be "Locomotive Breath" or "Aqualung." But you know what I can guarantee? I guarantee that you could listen all fucking day and not hear one song or one slight mention of Captain Beyond.

When I think back to all of the great, obscure bands of any genre that I love dearly, I clearly remember that they were those that were pointed out to me by either a close friend or the cool-ass, burnout, long-haired dude working at the record store. A friend once told me that the groups you hear on the radio are great bands, but the ones that you don't hear on the radio are usually the cream of the crop. They are those drowned in the wake of the bands that did achieve stardom but weren't necessarily better.

I was in my thirties when I got asked the question. The year was 2008. At that point in my life, I felt like I had pretty much heard it all. I wasn't really on a quest to discover new bands or to even put on my archaeological spectacles and go trudging for unearthed gems. I was completely happy with my musical options until a fateful day when a friend of mine named Wylie came into my office at work. At the time, I was toiling at the University of North Carolina at Chapel Hill as an IT Systems Administrator for the School of Education. I know, right? Blows your mind, huh? Don't believe me? Just look up that shit, and you'll find it. Where was I? Oh yeah, well, let me start another paragraph just in case Chuck Klosterman is reading this and calls me out for my shitty paragraph sculpting.

Anyway, my buddy Wylie comes into my office and asks, "Hey man, have you ever heard Captain Beyond?" As I shook my head and said, "No," a sparkle emitted from his eye, and a shit-eating grin took over his face. He said to me, "I'll hook you up. It'll blow your mind." Later that week, he gave me a burned copy of Captain Beyond's self-titled debut album. There was no artwork, no band photo, no liner notes, nothing. It was just a plain, old, silver top CDR with the name Captain Beyond scrawled out in Sharpie and the instructions "Smoke a joint and listen to this" written on the sleeve. Was this what Alice felt like when she saw the little bottle that said "Drink Me"?

In all honesty, I figured it was just another album a friend raved about that I would probably think was ok, or that I wouldn't like in the least. Kind of like how I was let down when I heard Frank Zappa after my friend James described him to me as some life-changing source. I mean, as we all know, music is subjective, so you have to take all of this with a grain of salt.

I didn't even rush to put on the Captain Beyond CD until one evening while my wife was out of town. She had gone to Washington, D.C for the summer to do a fellowship for grad school, and there I was, home alone. I sat down to clean out my laptop case, and there was the Captain Beyond CD just staring at me. After finishing my bachelor meal—a frozen DiGiorno pizza and a PBR tallboy, I packed the bowl, smoked up, and popped in the CD. I stretched out on the couch and prepared to be underwhelmed.

As the intro drum beats, courtesy of Bobby Caldwell, filled the cathedral ceiling of our Durham, North Carolina house, my interest was suddenly piqued. The minute the first verse of "Dancing Madly Backwards" began, my jaw hit the fucking floor. What the hell was I hearing? The sonic, cosmic riffs of Larry "Rhino" Reinhardt, the groove-laden bass lines of Lee Dorman, and the acid-fueled vocals of legendary Deep Purple singer Rod Evans. Good fucking God, what is this? The band slides right into "Armworth." *"What was my arm worth when they... took it away?"* Someone please get me a drip pan for my face... STAT! Whoa! What is this? Are they going back into "Dancing Madly Backwards"? Fuck me running!

I could barely wrap my head around what I was hearing. Every fucking time I thought I was getting it, another song would come out of nowhere and send me into this cosmic, ethereal frenzy. Song after song, the lyrical content floored me. "Mesmerization Eclipse" had

173

Evans singing, "*See the bright chipper in the harbor making iridescent waves. Need to try a little harder on the voyage to better days.*" Holy shit. Then all of a sudden, here comes Evans and Co. singing about the "Raging River of Fear": "*Raging River of Fear my friends is a-runnin' through us all… where it comes from and why it's here is a mystery to us all!*"

Every song topped the one before it, climaxing with what I consider to be the single greatest album closer of all time: "I Can't Feel Nothing (Part 1), As The Moon Speaks to the Sea, Astral Lady, As the Moon Speaks to the Sea (Return), I Can't Feel Nothin' (Part 2)." Yes, it's credited as five songs, but it is one of the single most epic suites I have ever heard. When "I Can't Feel Nothin' (Part 2)" brought it all back home to an end, I was pretty much left with my face on the floor and my head in the clouds, asking myself, "What the fuck just happened?" This album was pure fucking magic. It was unlike anything I had ever heard in my entire life, and honestly, I haven't heard anything like it since.

Captain Beyond did release one other fantastic album. The follow up was called *Sufficiently Breathless,* which is magical in its own right. But even as good as it is, it didn't come close to the level of pure, unbridled awesomeness of the debut. Captain Beyond's first record is so much more than a mere album. It's like unearthing a rare, precious talisman that has the power to change your life forever. This album changed my life because it showed me songwriting, creativity, and a performance with zero boundaries.

In 2018, I had the honor of becoming friends and working with legendary Captain Beyond drummer Bobby Caldwell when he decided to put together a new reincarnation of Captain Beyond. Getting to become friends with him over two years was amazing for

174

me. I told Bobby once that the first Captain Beyond album changed my life. When I told him the story you just read, he let out a hearty laugh and said, "Don. That's the effect that album was meant to have on people, and if that's how you experienced it, then we did our job."

The first Captain Beyond album is not one made to be skipped around or played on shuffle. Much like Pink Floyd's *Dark Side of the Moon, Captain Beyond* is a listening experience. Since the first time I heard it, I can't tell you how many people got a silver top CD-R from me with the words "Captain Beyond" scrawled on top of it in Sharpie. No artwork, no band photo, no liner notes, nothing. Captain Beyond is a band that I consider to be one of the greatest gifts a friend could give me, and it is a gift that I will continue giving for as long as I am breathing.

Pizza, whiskey, and dorking out over metal music.
Me and James recording Heavy Metal Lunch.
Durham, NC, 2008

Heavy Metal Lunch

In 2006, I was playing in a folk group called Shades of Winter in Durham, North Carolina. At our debut show as a duo, I was introduced to my singer Jen's friend and collaborator in her other band, Protean Mean. His name was James, and right away, we knew we were destined to be friends. I had heard from Jen that James was a huge Iron Maiden fan, and I was pumped to hear this. I burned a copy of the full *Maiden Japan* bootleg to CD and told Jen to give it to James. We eventually met at, of all things, a Festivus party, which was '80-themed. Of course, we both showed up decked out as '80s metalheads and pretty much spent the rest of the evening away from everyone else talking about metal.

James worked on the UNC-Chapel Hill campus, where I also worked, and eventually, he started working in the IT department. Every week (sometimes a few times a week), we would meet up for lunch. Sometimes it was at Joe's Joint, sometimes it was at Pepper's Pizza, and sometimes it was at Spanky's. Hell, sometimes it was just lunch in his office, but the ever-present conversation was Heavy Metal.

It was so much fun to have found a friend who understood my passion and love for Heavy Metal music. It also wasn't weird to him that I was this folk-singer dude whose favorite band was Iron Maiden because he wasn't far off from the same thing himself as an artist. Our lunches were so much fun and sometimes would stretch a bit more than an hour as we talked, ate, laughed, and argued over whether Saxon was any good or if "Screaming in the Night" by Krokus was indeed one of the greatest metal songs of all time. It was always a debate, sometimes a friendly argument, sometimes a total disagreement, but it was our time, and we dubbed it the Heavy Metal Lunch.

In 2007 or so, podcasts were a new thing. There weren't a whole lot of them out there, but at some point, we thought it would be cool to bring the Heavy Metal Lunch to life. James and I would congregate in my music studio garage, eat shitty food like pizza and Wendy's Baconators, drink beer and/or whiskey, and record ourselves talking about metal. We would talk about shit like our favorite debut albums, worst power ballads of all time, and sometimes, we would rap about anything at all. We even did a two-part episode on Heavy Metal 101. We developed a small fan base of about ten listeners (two of them were us) and would get messages from high school kids telling us how much they dug our podcast. We even received disturbingly awesome fan art.

Around this time, I also met a guy named Steve via my wife. Steve was all about metal, but he was into a lot of newer stuff. Well,

178

new at the time. He was all into bands like Mushroomhead, System of a Down, and Slipknot. There was one particular band that he listened to that caught my ear, and that was Lacuna Coil. I loved them because while they had a modern sound to them, they embodied a very old-school mentality. They put on amazing live shows, and I'm still a fan to this day. Steve opened my eyes and ears to giving more modern bands a chance. Even if I didn't like all of them, I never closed myself off to the idea of giving everyone a listen.

This was a great time for me because hanging out with James rekindled my long-time love for metal music. We inspired each other to hear things that we'd never paid much attention to. For instance, James turned me on to Bruce Dickinson's amazing solo catalog. I pretty much stopped listening to Bruce's stuff after *Balls to Picasso* because all of the reviews I read about *Skunkworks* was that he was going alternative. James proved me wrong, and I discovered a completely new collection of music that I had neglected. In exchange, I turned James on to the magic and mystical world of Ronnie James Dio-era Black Sabbath. Good things came out of this friendship, and to this day, even separated by the miles, we talk every day and continue to rag on each other, praise each other, and, most importantly, share our love of hard rock/metal music.

The Heavy Metal Lunch, hanging with James and Steve, and later discovering the New Wave of Traditional Heavy Metal would inspire me to launch the Great Southern Brainfart blog. If it hadn't been for these two dudes, I don't know that I would have ever had much interest in discovering this New Wave of Traditional Heavy Metal that would turn my life around and set me on a journalistic and musical path that I never thought I would take.

Hard rock mecca. Me at the Rainbow Bar and Grill.
Los Angeles, CA, 2010

Goin' to California

Like many my age, I grew up a fan of the Los Angeles and Hollywood hard rock and metal scene, with bands like Mötley Crüe, RATT, Dokken, and Poison. In their prime, they were the kings of the Sunset Strip, but before that, each was merely one of a slew of unknowns that roamed the Strip handing out flyers, trying to get folks to check out their gigs at venues like Whiskey A-Go-Go, The Roxy, Gazzarri's, and the Troubadour.

Growing up in New Orleans, I would daydream about these legendary venues that seemed an entire world away. I'd imagine what it would be like on a Friday night, walking up and down the strip handing out flyers to hot chicks, playing to packed houses of screaming fans, and then partying like a debaucherous rock star at the Rainbow Bar and Grill until the wee hours of the morning. I would lose myself in these fantasies for hours as I lay in my bedroom with the headphones on and blasting "Out of the Cellar" or "Shout at the Devil." As I got older, I no longer dreamt of pounding the pavement to hand out gig flyers, but I still always wanted to see where it all happened.

In November 2009, I got my opportunity. My sister-in-law and her family live out there, and after being invited to visit, I excitedly accepted and made my way to California. The week before my trip, I carefully planned out my "Don's Day in Hollywood" and figured out what I wanted to see and do. My awesome sister-in-law loaned me her car, and I made my way down the 101 for my Hollywood adventure.

Most of you who are reading this might be thinking, "Dude, why did you go during the day? Nothing is going on because everything happens at night, brah!" Well, that's just why. I had no real desire to take in the nightlife or to see shows at any of the venues. This was a soul journey. It wasn't about trying to party or live the life of a washed-up rocker for a night. It was just about me taking in the vibe and the spirit of the city in the light of day.

My first stop was the Rock Walk at Hollywood's Guitar Center. Just walking up to the awning of the store gave me goosebumps. I made my rounds checking out all the handprints. I was giddy with excitement when I saw Ronnie James Dio's prints, and right away had to take a selfie with them. Iron Maiden's included prints from their legendary mascot, Eddie the 'Ed, and Ozzy Osbourne guitarist Zakk Wylde's prints had not just his hands but his beer can as well. Motorhead's prints featured Lemmy's signature middle finger, and Def Leppard's included Rick Allen's foot, which I found to be pretty humorous because after losing his left arm in a 1984 car accident, Allen has been playing drums using both of his feet and one arm.

While I was there, I figured I'd pick up some guitar strings since I needed some for a gig back home in Atlanta the following week. I had a great time just browsing the guitars and talking to one of the sales guys. He told me about his band (I forgot their name) and that playing at the Whisky a Go-Go isn't all that it's cracked up to be as it can be "pay to play," where bands have to "pay" to play a venue. Usually, a band is given 50-100 tickets and told to sell them for a set price. The tickets that don't get sold are then paid for by the band out of pocket. The Guitar Center dude was super cool and even gave me great directions to my next stops down the road.

I found a pay lot a bit down on Sunset Boulevard, so I pulled in and paid five bucks for an unlimited time. Score! I gathered my bag and camera and started walking down Sunset. Right away, I could feel the energy of this part of town. I imagined what it must have looked like at night back then, with hordes of longhaired dudes walking up and down the sidewalk handing out flyers to their upcoming shows with hopes of being the next big thing out of California. As I made my way down the road, I saw The Roxy, the Whiskey A-Go-Go, and the Rainbow Bar and Grill. This was it! This was the block where many of my favorite bands played some of their most legendary shows. This was where Van Halen was discovered, this was where Mötley Crüe played, and this was where The Doors not only played but were signed. What an amazing thing it was to see these historic venues. I looked in the windows, took pictures of the marquees, and took in the vibe and spirit of these places.

With a rumbling in my tummy, I strolled over to the Rainbow Bar & Grill. It was about noon, and I was the only one there. I walked into the restaurant. I ended up chatting with the manager, and he was a very cool guy. I told him my little soul-searching story and that it was my first visit ever to Hollywood. He was so kind, and he took me on a tour of this legendary establishment. He pointed out all the places where all the famous people hang out inside. I saw the place where Guns N Roses filmed a scene for their "November Rain" video, and I got to see where Ronnie James Dio often sat and enjoyed a meal with friends. He told me to take my time and check out all the pictures on the walls. I could feel the spirits of those long gone and those that still linger. The Rainbow was a truly magical place.

After some time, I made my way to the outside patio bar and got to see the place where Lemmy of Motorhead would frequently hang out playing video poker while drinking Jack & Coke (now called a Lemmy in his honor since he passed in 2015). I approached the bar and pulled up a chair where I was one of three people. I was greeted by my bartender who introduced herself as "Kat with a K." She recommended the cheeseburger and fries, which I got, along with a cold Rolling Rock, to wash it down.

Kat told me that even though she likes the crazy nights, the quiet day shifts are sometimes a nice change for her. She told me how she moved to Hollywood with her boyfriend, who was a musician, and that they had recently split up. I asked her if she'd ever considered moving back home. She took a deep breath with eyes closed, sighed happily, and said, "I'm in Hollywood, babe. No fucking way." Before too long, my burger and fries came out. Being known as a rowdy party place full of debauchery, I didn't have high expectations for the food, but my lunch was surprisingly amazing. As I finished my meal and beer, I felt like I had succeeded in taking in all that I had hoped to. I came, I saw, and I conquered a kick-ass burger. I picked up a Rainbow Bar & Grill t-shirt and thanked Kat and the manager for their awesome company.

I will never forget that day in Hollywood. I paid homage to the greats and the spirits of those who were left behind. As I walked back to the car with a smile on my face, I felt like a void in my life had been filled, like all those years dreaming and wondering about what it was like could finally be replaced with experience. Ok, so I didn't get to play these places or bang a ton of hot groupies, but I did get to see the Strip firsthand as I'd always dreamed of doing. Hollywood, I learned, truly does have a heart. You've just got to poke around.

Check out my blog!
www.TheGreatSouthernBrainfart.com

Start Your Own Damn Blog

In 2009, my wife and I moved back to Atlanta, Georgia. It had been nearly ten years since we'd been away, and we were coming back to what looked and felt like a whole new city. Atlanta was changing dramatically, and gentrification was taking over. What were once shady, industrial parts of town had been converted into expensive lofts, douche bag wine bars, craft beer houses, and overpriced burger joints. But the concert nightlight was as alive as it ever was. Some of long-standing venues, like the Masquerade, Smith's Olde Bar, and Variety Playhouse, were still thriving and there were new clubs, like the Earl, the 529, and the Drunken Unicorn that provided space for touring bands, as well as local artists.

Once we settled in, I guess you can say that I was pretty much living the dream. After many years of long hours and hard work in graduate school, my wife received her Ph.D. and got her dream job. She looked to me and said, "Hey, it's your turn now to do whatever you want. Pursue your passions and live your dreams." I mean, how fucking cool was that? For me, this was an opportunity to do just what she said, to pursue some things that I always wanted to do but couldn't afford because it either didn't pay jack shit or I was just too busy to do anything else.

I started volunteering for a local non-profit organization doing entry-level computer training for volunteers and community members. It was fun at first, but then it got to be just as much of a hassle as working a paying job; eventually, I just said, "Fuck this" and gave it up. I toyed with the idea of working part-time in the IT field again, but working part-time and getting there and getting home and blah blah blah just wouldn't have been worth it, so a domestic god I became. I loved my role, and I still love it. I kick ass at cleaning bathrooms, I love doing yard work, and I can make a mean ass meatloaf, so I guess you could say that I'm a catch. But something was missing. What was it that I wanted to do?

I had been loosely keeping a music blog since 2007 or so, and I always enjoyed it. The blog had no rhyme or reason, structure, or identity. It was me talking about music. I talked about my favorite Phish shows, shitty Phish show and some of my favorite bands like the Allman Brothers Band, Lacuna Coil, and Iron Maiden. I would write little essays and even sometimes do interviews with random bands. I had started reading a lot of hard rock/metal blogs after we moved, including Blabbermouth, Brave Words and Bloody Knuckles, and Metal Sucks and saw that the kind of metal music that I loved so much as a young man was making somewhat of a comeback. This got me excited but also kind of pissed me off.

188

I would read these blogs where they praised the new Guns N' Roses lineup, yet I would listen to them, and thought they fucking sucked. They would rave about bands like Arch Enemy and the latest Slayer album, and again, I would be so disappointed and find myself saying, "What is everyone hearing that I'm not?" Then I would hear the new RATT album (yes, RATT made an awesome album in the '00s called *Infestation*) and wonder why nobody was talking about it. I remembered this old Drivin' N Cryin' shirt I had many years ago that said, "Start Your Own Damn Band." Well, I took that motto and applied it here. If you don't like what you're reading, start your own damn blog. That is when the Great Southern Brainfart was truly born.

Now I had a mission, a goal. But where the fuck to start? I took to the internet to find the names of the press people who handled the bands I liked. And I'm here to tell you, most people will ignore your emails, but it just takes a few people to believe in you. I reached out to Roadrunner Records, who was working the RATT album, and corresponded with Amy Sciarretto and Lily Ryden. These two women were so awesome, and they must have seen something in me that the other publicists didn't. They started by sending me a box of CDs to check out. I had never heard of many of the artists, bands like Killswitch Engage and Opeth. Some piqued my interest and some not so much (I'm talking to you, Slipknot), but nonetheless, this was the beginning. I wrote a few album reviews on my new blog, and I must have done ok because I maintained a relationship with the record label.

The next person who took the time to work with me was Jon Freeman. Jon runs his PR firm, Freeman Promotions, and he worked with some acts that he thought would be great fits for my blog and for what I was into. Jon connected me with the great Axel Rudi Pell, Riotgod, Lucifer, and a slew of other bands, which was an amazing experience. This was another example of how someone took a chance on me and believed in what I was trying to do. To this day, we have an amazing bond and continue to work together on everyone from Hardline to Monster Magnet to GWAR and many bands in between.

Nuclear Blast is, without a doubt, the big fucking shark in the tank when it comes to metal labels. It started as a label to the heaviest of the heavy, but then they saw a change in the current; a lot of amazing European bands were coming forward, leading a whole new revolution of music. Their PR person at the time, Loana Valencia, was someone I was corresponding with. She had turned me on to bands such as Kadavar, Blues Pills, Avantasia, and Blind Guardian, to name a few.

One day, Loana called me on the phone and said, "Don, I just heard your new favorite band. They're a pretty new band out of Sweden, and I'd love for you to do an interview and review of their latest album." That album was *Hisingen Blues* by Graveyard. She was right. I loved their classic hard rock sound and they quickly became one of my favorite bands. And Loana became a mentor, offering advice and encouraging me to use my voice as a writer. She liked my writing, and I loved her passion for working with her bands, so we struck up a bond that lasts to this day. She turned me on to bands such as Scorpion Child, Epica, and Municipal Waste, all bands that I still love passionately.

In 2015, I got turned on to a book called *Louder Than Hell: An Oral History of Metal,* written by Jon Wiederhorn and former *RIP Magazine* writer Katherine Turman. Without even knowing it, I had been a fan of Katherine's for some time, reading many of her pieces in *RIP Magazine*. When I interviewed her that year, I felt this connection to her as a writer. We struck up a friendship and she somewhat became the Lester Bangs to my William Miller. Over the years, Katherine has served as a mentor to me and has been there to challenge and push me as a writer, urging me to try things outside of my comfort zone. You know, like writing a book.

As the years passed and the hours bent, my blog developed an identity of its own. The Great Southern Brainfart became synonymous with being a site that tells it like it is without holding back. Whether it violently pisses off Sebastian Bach, gets me banned from Guns N' Roses shows, or has bands patting me on the back and welcoming me in as family, I have taken a stance of being unmerciful, honest, and unabridged (with some shitty grammar thrown in). Without people like Amy, Lilly, Jon, Loana, and Katherine, I wouldn't be the writer that I am today.

I continue to grow day by day, essay by essay, and review by review. I still call on these people from time to time for some guidance, and it always blows me away that they're still there for me. After nearly ten years of doing The Great Southern Brainfart, I have created something that is mine. It is my soapbox, my lunchroom table, my corner booth at the diner, or whatever else you want to describe it as. This blog is my voice, my opinion, and my undying truth, so if you don't like it, start your own damn blog

"If anyone on my friends list supports a troll by the name of Don de Leaumont and his 'The Great Southern Brainfart' webzine, I'd beg you to reconsider your support of him."

"What a crock of shit. When your press cred has the word 'fart' in it you should be banned from everything."

"I've never forgiven him for putting out one of his little hit pieces on the day my dog died. We've had repeated discussions about putting sugar in his gas tank and slashing his tires."

"That guy has deserved to gargle razorblades for a while now, but shit. May he now gargle them and then be struck by a bus."

Actual quotes from people who don't like me
because of my honest, unfiltered opinions.

The Occupational Hazard
of Being Me

"Hey! Aren't you The Great Southern Brainfart?" When I am out at a show and someone comes up to me and asks this question, my chest gets just a tad tight as I prepare for one of two things: a hell yeah high five or a punch in the kisser. As you all know, I'm not shy or filtered when it comes to my true, honest feelings about a band. If I love them, I say so. If I think they're just "ok," I say so. If I think they fucking suck, well, I say so. There's nothing more to it than that.

I know that by being this brutally honest, I am putting myself out there not only as someone my readers can respect and appreciate, but someone who pisses off quite a few bands. You all probably remember the now-infamous "deBACHle" where Sebastian Bach had a few choice words for me via Facebook after I gave him a shitty concert review after he gave a shitty concert. That was a good example of an artist who was not too happy with my negative review of his band's show.

In a lot of ways, I guess you could say it was an honor to be threatened with bodily harm by Sebastian Bach. I've had Guns N' Roses completely blacklist me from their press list because of negative reviews, and again, that's fine. But being confronted face to face by an angered band member that I talked smack about, that's a whole different level of scary, like Wes Craven level scary.

One night, I was out and about at the 120 Tavern in Atlanta to take in a performance by my good friends/NWOTHM veterans Widow. I was at the bar with their guitarist Chris when out of nowhere, I was approached by a very tall, scary, and seemingly intoxicated individual. He gets in my face and goes, "Hey! Aren't you the Great Southern Brainfart?" Ok, so this is where that feeling comes in, but this time around, I knew it wasn't going to end with a high five. It was going to probably end with a dinner consisting of a knuckle sandwich and a side of my own teeth.

So there I was face to face with this guy. "Hey! Aren't you the Great Southern Brainfart?"

"Yeah, that's me," I replied.

He looks at me with his face getting red in anger and says, "Man, you said that we were the worst band in Atlanta, man. That was pretty fucking shitty of you to say that."

I just looked at him and said very honestly, "What band are you in?"

He looked somewhat perplexed and said, "I'm in Brazen Angel."

I had to think for a second, and when I remembered them, I replied, "Hey, man. I said that a *long* time ago. Don't worry, plenty of bands have taken that title from you since then." He just stared me down, and I figured at any moment that knuckle sandwich was coming, but then Chris pulled him aside to get a few pictures with them for Widow's Facebook page. I used the opportunity to make a brisk exit to safety.

The next day, I had to go on my website, search their name, and see just what I'd said about them. It turns out I *did* say that they were the worst band in Atlanta by awarding them Worst Local Band on my 2012 Farty Awards. I was pretty harsh, but I was 100% honest, and I still stand by my opinions on Brazen Angel. Since that post, I have seen them another two times and never said another thing about them, figuring, "Why flog a dead horse?"

It will never cease to amaze me how some artists are completely unable to receive or accept any negative criticism in the press. What are you going to do? Punch the teeth in of every person who gives you a bad review? In my opinion, there is nothing more pompous and arrogant than someone who gets angry enough to actually come close to physical violence over a bad review. As an artist myself, I know that not everything I do will be liked or even appreciated by everyone. Those who have negative things to say about my work— my writing or my music—I take a moment to analyze, process it, and then decide if said information is worth consideration or if it's just something that I can ball up and toss into the mental trashcan for a three-pointer.

When people get angry at me for negative reviews, my first thought is that they must believe, in some small way that I'm right, and that the ugly truth is something they cannot accept. More than anything, I felt bad for Brazen Angel dude since he had clearly been brewing in him for four years. That can't be good for the body, mind, or soul. At the end of it all, just let it go. Regardless, now, when I hear someone say, "Hey! Aren't you The Great Southern Brainfart?" I will still tighten up and flinch, but I will stand by my words until something changes my mind. That, my friends, is the truth, and as they say, "the truth hurts"… literally.

Beard envy much?
Me and Styx vocalist/keyboardist Lawrence Gowan.
Alpharetta, GA, 2019

Making a Connection: Learning the Art of the Interview

Without a doubt, one of my favorite things to do is interview musicians. I fucking love it. This is where I get to be Riki Rachtman. This is where I get to be Katherine Turman. This is where I get to be the person I always dreamed of being. I get to be the guy who decides just what to ask these artists, and I can control how deep or shallow the conversation goes.

The whole idea of an essay on this topic almost escaped me for this book. Until this morning. I rolled out of bed around 10:45 a.m. and said, "Shit. I have an interview with Randy Jackson of Zebra at 11:30!" I jumped up, washed my face, brewed a cup of coffee, and made my way down to the basement, still in my PJs and smelling like ass. I got out my trusty digital recorder, pulled out my list of questions, put in my earpiece microphone, put on my headset, and was calling Randy Jackson at 11:32.

For the next fifty minutes or so, Randy and I talked like we were hanging out in his kitchen up in Long Island, having coffee. We talked about the New Orleans music scene, why Zebra migrated to New York, and whatnot. At the end, he thanked me for a fun interview and said, "I enjoy talking to you, Don. It's always fun." That right there is what it's all about as far as I'm concerned. It's all about making that connection, and when it's made, it's the best fucking high you can imagine.

I don't know if it's because I'm such a uber dork fan of certain artists, but my goal for interviewing these people is to, hopefully, give them an experience that isn't like the other twenty interviews they might have to do that day. I know they are often exhausted during a day of back-to-back interviews, so I try my hardest to stick out from the pack. I want them not to feel like they have to dredge through another thirty-minute interview. I want them actually to *enjoy* it.

For the most part, I have been very successful with my interviews, and the more I do it, the better I get at it. Even early on, I remember thinking to myself, "Talk to this person like you would if you just met them at a bar." I interviewed former Megadeth drummer Shawn Drover once backstage. I remember being introduced to him, and while he was very nice, he didn't look like he wanted to be there. Still, we just started talking, and all of a sudden, I saw his body language loosening up. He uncrossed his arms, leaned in when answering questions, and laughed, and I felt like I had made a connection. He even showed me the practice kit he uses to warm up and took a few photos with me. That was one of those moments where I felt like I truly began to come into my own as an interviewer.

Another favorite interview of mine was with, of all people, Lawrence Gowen, the singer/keyboardist for Styx. Now the average metalhead might think, "Styx? Really?" Without a doubt, Lawrence has been one of my favorite people to interview. I have had the pleasure of speaking with him twice so far, and every time, it's a fucking blast. Our first interview had us making a connection as people and over our love of Heavy Metal and other styles of music. Almost a year later, we did a second interview and he told me how much he had been looking forward to it. He's a really funny guy and a big metal fan. One of his favorites is the European extreme metal band Dimmu Borgir. It's kind of crazy when the singer for Styx's favorite band is heavier than anything you listen to as a metal blogger. It's always a fun conversation, and it's a great example of how the connection keeps carrying on from interview to interview.

Whenever I have an interview coming up, one of the first things I do is hop online and start reading and watching them do other interviews. Right away, it's easy to see what questions these people get asked over and over. You can see the boredom on their faces, and you can read and hear by the overall tone of their one-line answers that they are not engaged. My strategy is *not* to ask those same questions. And in fact, one of my favorite questions to open with is, "What question do you get asked so much that if you hear it again, you'll scream?" That usually breaks the ice. They laugh and usually say something like, "When I get asked, 'how's the tour going?'" We'll laugh, and then from there, it'll just be a great conversation.

When I'm interviewing artists, I want to know more about them than what they may share in the average interview. For instance, I loved learning that Exodus drummer Tom Hunting is a huge Journey fan. I found it super interesting that Municipal Waste

201

vocalist Tony Foresta is a big fan of Canadian indie pop band Tegan and Sara. I also loved learning that if given the opportunity, Cinderella's Tom Keifer would play in The Rolling Stones for just one night. I enjoyed debating with former Queensryche singer Geoff Tate about the band's album *Promised Land*. He stated that he didn't like it, and I told him it was my favorite. He asked why, I shared my reasons with him, and he seemed genuinely intrigued by my answer.

One of my all-time favorite connections in an interview was with Jordan Rudess of Dream Theater. The band on their tour, *A Dramatic Tour of Events,* which was the first tour to feature new drummer Mike Mangini. I watched and read so many interviews with Jordan, and, of course, every question he was asked was about Mike Mangini. I noticed that in almost none of the interviews was Jordan asked about his material as an artist or his work in developing some cool music apps for iPads and whatnot. I decided to use this as my edge and began doing my homework.

When it came time for my interview with Jordan, I was told that I had fifteen minutes with him and that at the twelve-minute-mark, I would be signaled by the manager that it was time to wind things up. Jordan came into the room backstage at the Tabernacle. He was very mellow and seemed to be a pretty shy guy. The first thing I told him was that I didn't want to talk about Mike Mangini and that I wanted to talk more about him and his music and interests. His face lit up in a smile, he and said, "We can definitely do that."

We started talking about how he got into music, what he listened to in order to wind down after a show, and his cool music apps. At the twelve-minute-mark, I realized we hadn't covered most of the questions I had for him. His manager came in and gave me the cue, and Jordan said, "I'm having fun with this one. We're good."

Forty-five minutes later, we ended the interview, and a connection was made that exists to this day.

Sometimes the interviews don't always go as well as I'd like them to from my end. I once interviewed Floor Jansen while she was on tour with her band Revamp. During the interview, I realized how little I knew of the most current Revamp album and found myself stumbling with questions. I could sense a bit of her frustration, but she was kind, and honestly, I hadn't done my homework for this one. I also had a really bad interview with Testament guitarist Eric Peterson. He seemed uninterested in talking to me. He even mentioned that he was hungover and that he'd rather not be doing interviews. Instead of trying harder to engage him, I just gave up and let it crash and burn. Both of these interviews presented me with valuable lessons on how important it is always to be prepared with your questions and to know that not all interviews will be great ones.

Beyond just making a connection during an interview, I've been lucky to become friends with some of the people I've interviewed. Now I'm sure there are journalism classes that devote entire lectures on why you shouldn't do this. In fact, there's a website that has a list of "The 50 Rules of Good Journalism" with #43 listed as "You can be friendly with someone you report on, but you can never be their friend." I disagree. I think it's only a problem if the friendship causes you to censor yourself. And I have no problem calling out a band if they put out something shitty, even if they are a friend.

But that being said, I realize that not all artists want to create a personal connection with someone they consider the press. There was a scene in *Almost Famous* where young journalist William Miller is called "the enemy" by the band he's trying to interview. And earlier in the movie, Lester Bangs tells William, in a nutshell, not to make friends with the rock stars because they only like you while you're inflating their egos and the minute you aren't, they'll drop you like a bad habit. Unfortunately, I had that experience with the singer of White Wizzard after I gave their 2018 comeback album *Infernal Overdrive* a bad review. Next day, he unfriended me from Facebook. Look, I get it and I don't need to be friends with everyone. But I am thankful to the bands who have respected me and maintained friendships (if not friendly relationships) even after I've said something brutally honest that they may not have wanted to hear.

My Journey Down the Psych/Occult Rock Rabbit Hole

WARNING: this essay may have been written while under the influence of marijuana. Proceed with caution.

In May 2014, I began to notice a common thread that tied some of my new favorite bands together. Bands such as Jess and the Ancient Ones, Purson, Lucifer, and Graveyard all fell into the genre of psych/occult rock. Once I recognized the link, down the rabbit hole I went to try to find out what exactly it was about this music that struck such a massive chord with me.

Maybe it is the mystical vibe that surrounds the overall makeup of these bands' songs. The way these bands approach their music is so much more subtle than their peers. What they lack in piercing volume, they make up for with great lyrics and music that flows from heavy to mellow. The vocals are crisp and soulful while the lyrics are enunciated so you can understand every word sung. It's an element that I never got out of Death Metal. You're supposed to be evil and scary. How am I supposed to be scared or intrigued when I can't understand a single word being sung?

There are occult/psych-rock bands on the scene that aren't anywhere near as musically heavy as the more intense Black and Death Metal. These bands are musically reminiscent of the '60s and '70s psychedelic rock, with dark and thought-provoking lyrics expressing their dark spiritual beliefs. Songs like this captivate me, intrigue me, and at times creep me out. In my opinion, nobody does it better in this genre than Jess and The Ancient Ones.

Out of Finland, Jess and the Ancient Ones clawed their way through the scene, making a name for themselves as the hand-picked support act for King Diamond's 2014 North American tour. With a sound that is a fine mix of Jefferson Airplane, Iron Butterfly, and some Dick Dale surf guitar in there for good measure, Jess and the Ancient Ones rose higher than the others because of the lyrics. The ethereal and soulful voice of Jess, along with the well-crafted, intriguing lyrics and music of Thomas Corpse, is what created the perfect package for me. Lyrically I felt as if I was reading some esoteric sacred text:

> *"From the shadows, you have come*
> *To stand across the path of the sun*
> *Everlasting secrets that you keep*
> *Revealed for those who dare to seek*
> *In the gardens of dark matter*
> *The serpents coil and twist*
> *As they bind their tails*

Around the eternal pillars"

I don't know about you, but to me, that's every bit as haunting and creepy as just about any other bloody guts screaming death metal band. I think this music drew me in because it offered an alternative to the loud, in-your-face, over-the-top Heavy Metal without sacrificing the hard edge and the darker side of hard rock/metal.

The late '60s and early/mid-'70s yielded some of the most obscure, understated, unique, and groundbreaking occult/psych-rock bands. Most were left to dwell in a vortex of obscurity, left behind in the dust by bands that broke through the mainstream. Many of these bands' albums lie buried like fine gems waiting to be unearthed. It was downright overwhelming discovering how many of these fucking cool but mostly forgotten bands existed.

How in Satan's name was I even supposed to find what I wanted in this cornucopia of obscurity? Instead of taking it upon myself to try and comb through the bands that were out there, I figured the best thing to do would be to start talking to the modern bands I loved and ask them about their influences. Rosie Cunningham and Sam Robinson of Purson revealed to me just how much they were inspired by bands like Soft Machine, Hawkwind, and an obscure German band called Amon Düül II. Jess and the Ancient Ones and Lucifer named bands like Coven, Shocking Blue, and 13th Floor Elevators as influences. Lucifer lead vocalist Johanna Sadonis made me aware of a classic occult band called Black Widow. Wucan and Kadavar introduced me to krautrock (German psychedelic rock which I didn't even know was a thing), and long conversations on the tour bus with Graveyard opened me up to Peter Green era Fleetwood Mac.

As I ventured into these mystical waters, I found myself completely enthralled and immersed in the music I was finding. I was fascinated by the progressive and, at times, psychedelic nature of these bands and the haunting, mystical, and flat-out the sacrilegious subject matter of their songs. We had Coven from the U.S. performing with a more hard rock kind of sound; they even performed a full-on Black Mass on their album *Witchcraft Reaps & Destroys Minds*. Amon Düül II had elements of both Jess and the Ancient Ones and Purson with its melodic, ethereal, and fuzz-driven guitar. Then we have Black Widow from the U.K., who played with a more progressive nature, which released the album *Sacrifice* with lyrics such as:

> *"I conjure thee. I conjure thee. I conjure thee to appear.*
> *I raise you mighty demon. Come before me join me here.*
> *Lucifer"*

If that wasn't enough, Black Widow appeared on the German music television show *The Beat Club* and performed the *Sacrifice* album in its entirety, including an intro of a very eerie incantation before ending with a mock sacrifice of a young woman. I can't even begin to imagine how extreme and intense this was to witness on television. I wish I could see how the people in the '70s reacted to this.

My journey down the psych/occult rock rabbit hole continues. As I write this, I am venturing into a whole plethora of bands such as May Blitz, Leafhound, and Bang, to name a few. People, the "related artists" button on Spotify has become my "burnout record store guy." As I click on each band, a whole handful of other bands are presented that keeps beckoning me further and further into the depths and asking, "How did I never heard of this?"

What I have come to discover while embarking on this journey is that it never ends. It also reminds me of how many great, obscure bands are lying there waiting to be unearthed by curious minds. As always, if you want to see the full greatness of things truly, dig below the surface and look and listen with new, heightened senses. Dig, brothers and sisters. Dig. As you seek, so shall you find.

Happy Birthday to us!
Me and a *Dark Side of the Moon* mural.
Tucker, GA, 2018

Dark Side of the Moon & Me: Turning 40 Together

Some people consider hitting the big 4-0 the beginning of the end; it's over the hill. And in 2013, I was about to be over that hill. I have no problems with aging, and this particular birthday, I was honored to be sharing a milestone in life with one of the single greatest albums of all time: Pink Floyd's *Dark Side of the Moon*. If you're reading this, chances are you own *Dark Side of the Moon* or at least owned it at one time. It's a timeless album that was truly lightning captured in a bottle.

In some ways, I guess you could say that we grew up together. I first heard *Dark Side of the Moon* back in the summer before ninth grade in 1988. I had heard Pink Floyd songs on the radio and was familiar with the "hits" like "Another Brick in the Wall," "Comfortably Numb," and even their more current (at the time) hits like "Learning to Fly" and "Dogs of War." One day while listening to the radio, I heard the song "Time." At that moment, I wasn't sure why, but for some odd reason, it struck a chord with me. It was enough to move me to pick up the album, and what I heard was much more than an album full of songs. It was a new life companion that would see me through many ups and downs.

Listening to *Dark Side of the Moon* was more intense than anything this fourteen-year-old had ever experienced, and let me tell you, I couldn't get enough of it. The opening track, "Speak to Me," filled me with anticipation and a sense of anxiety. It made me feel like I was helplessly falling at a high speed. When "Breathe in the Air" entered with that beautiful first chord, it felt like a parachute had opened. I was peacefully and very slowly alternating between ascending and descending, never sure when I would touch the ground.

The gentle slide and rhythm guitar filled my heart and soul full of air. Guitarist/vocalist David Gilmour seemed to be able to pick single notes out of the air to the point where I could almost see them being plucked like berries from a tree. Rick Wright's beautiful and subtle keyboard playing and backing vocals complimented the soothing voice of Gilmour while bassist Roger Waters and drummer Nick Mason created a soft foundation that felt like it could have been a huge foam cushion to break my fall without the slightest bit of jarring. This is a heavy fucking thing to be able to feel for a kid whose life revolved around W.A.S.P, Twisted Sister, and Iron Maiden.

"Time" really hit me and touched a nerve. *"Digging away the hours that make up a dull day."* This was me with every passing, hot, sweltering New Orleans summer day. I had nothing to do, and I was bored to tears. *"Tired of lying in the sunshine. Staying home to watch the rain. You are young, and life is long, and there is time to kill today."* I

212

realized as a young boy that while life is short, I found myself in a hurry to become an adult. I didn't like being a kid, and I didn't hear this as a piece of knowledge but more so the fact that I related to the idea of hating the sun and loving the rain.

The older I get, the more I find myself understanding the message behind "Time" and relating to the overall message within the lyrics. While I am still tired of the sunshine and love the rain, I'm getting older, and there isn't that much time to kill anymore. I have to make the best of every minute I have left in this cosmos.

The soaring up and down musical and vocal dynamics of "The Great Gig in the Sky" make me think that this is what it must be like to leave this plane when one dies. While I don't believe in God, I sometimes wonder what becomes of our spirit after we're gone. If passing over is anything like this song, I am not so afraid of it.

"Us and Them" is a song that, unfortunately, remains relevant, even decades later. While it is a sad testament of the fucked-up situation our world is in under horrible dictatorship (yes, in America) and a severe global climate crisis, "Us and Them," to me, is a beacon of hope that comforts me while still making me aware of the shit that is going on around me and what I can to make a change.

"Money" didn't mean much to young Don other than it was a badass song. It had a cool tempo change and one of the most recognizable bass lines in rock music. Older Don, on the other hand, got the meaning behind "Money." Money is something we rely on for survival, and while many people barely scrape by in life, there is a lot of greed and selfishness among the wealthy and powerful. It's a hard concept to grasp when you're a kid anticipating your $5.00 a week allowance, but as a working adult, it is a song that is sadly accurate in the reality of what money is and what it does to our world, both good and bad.

Dark Side of the Moon never sounds dated or played out. Every listen is as exciting as the first time I heard it. It is an album full of meanings and messages that get clearer and more relatable the older I get. I feel like I never stop learning and connecting with this album. I have to wonder sometimes if Pink Floyd even had a clue of the life-changing impact *Dark Side of the Moon* would have on many others like myself.

Since 1988, I have owned six—count 'em, SIX—copies of *Dark Side of the Moon*: two cassettes, two vinyl copies that were permanently borrowed, one copy on CD that I still own to this day, and the holy grail: a complete copy on vinyl including the posters and sticker inserts. It's one of those albums that once you own and truly listen to, it becomes a part of your life.

I retreat to *Dark Side of the Moon* frequently. When life seems to get a little too heavy for me, I put it on to loosen the load. It's also great in the background over a nice, chill dinner with my wife, and it takes me into a dream state when I lie down at night to go to sleep. *Dark Side of the Moon* is a musical chameleon as it adapts to whatever mood or situation I need it to be a part of, and it will forever be a huge part of my life.

Dark Side of the Moon and I have been through a lot. Together, we've moved eight times, had five girlfriends, got married, got stoned for the first time, taken countless road trips, and had countless nights alone. We've flown from Georgia to London and back and crossed paths in restaurants and bars. *Dark Side of the Moon* and I have had many experiences together and somehow managed to come through it all unscathed.

As I type this very essay, *Dark Side of the Moon* is playing in the background, and that beautifully quiet part at the end of "Great Gig in the Sky" just came on. I had to pause what I was doing to take it in. I closed my eyes, listened, and felt it. On a rainy, gloomy winter's day, *Dark Side of the Moon* is helping to inspire the words you are reading right now. On this day, *Dark Side of the Moon* was my muse, yet another role of many that this amazing record plays for me.

Holding court backstage with King Crimson
lead singer/guitarist Jakko Jakszyk.
Atlanta, GA, 2019

In the Court of King Crimson

For nearly ten years, my best friend James has been trying to get me into King Crimson. King Crimson is, without a doubt, "his" band, and he did his level best to turn me on to them. I tried. I did. I listened to the albums. I tried *Red* and *Court of the Crimson King*, and I tried listening to various songs and live performances. For some reason or another, nothing seemed to click. I didn't hate it, but I didn't love it. There was just something keeping me from truly connecting with the music. I never wrote them off completely, but I just chalked it up to me not getting it and figured that it was something over my head. However, all of that was about to change.

James was super pumped when it was announced that King Crimson would be hitting the road for a pretty rare, full-on North American tour, with a stop in Atlanta. James insisted that I go to the show with him so much so that he bought me a ticket! Who am I to turn down a free concert? To get myself somewhat prepared, I opened Spotify and found the album *Radical Action to Unseat the Hold of Monkey Mind*. It's a live album that was released in 2016, featuring a lineup that has been together (give or take a member or two) since 2014. While listening to this album, something started to happen. Maybe it was a new vocalist/guitarist Jakko Jakszyk, or maybe it was because I was excited to see them live with my best friend, but I started to feel something, a connection of sorts that I hadn't felt in previous attempts at listening. This made me even more excited to take in King Crimson in concert.

King Crimson wants their fans to experience to "enjoy the concert with your eyes and your ears." There are huge signs on either side of the stage stating that if you take pictures or video of the show, you'd be escorted out. What I think they really mean, is that if you take pictures, King Crimson guitarist and founding member Robert Fripp might come down from the stage and suck the soul out of your body through your ear and mash it into putty right before your eyes. Honestly, I loved seeing these signs because I can't tell you how sick I get of having to look at the screen of people's phones in front of me as they capture shitty quality video to post on YouTube for nobody to see.

The band opened with "Larks' Tongues in Aspic (Part 1)," and right away, I could feel myself being drawn into this mystical world. The stage was lined with three drummers, all of whom played an integral part in each composition, which alone was mind-blowing to see. Fripp himself is like Oz, only instead of hiding behind a curtain, he's all like, "I'm Oz, bitch. See and fear me!"

Watching that man command the King Crimson vessel was mesmerizing. Tony Levin is a musical beast. He grooved out with all his toys, (bass, upright bass, Chapman Stick, Funk Fingers, etc.). The real game-changer, for me, was lead vocalist/guitarist Jakko Jakszyk.

Turns out that Jakko was the missing piece of the puzzle that was keeping me from truly "seeing" the whole thing, and I was so fucking excited that I had finally "got it."

Jakko's vocal work on songs like "Pictures of a City," "Easy Money," and "The Letters" absolutely blew me out of the cosmos. Have you ever had one of those moments when you hear a certain piece of music performed and it just grabs your heart and tugs on it so hard that every muscle in your body sends this feeling of warmth that then leads to tears? I had this very experience while hearing stellar performances of "Starless," "Epitaph," and "Court of the Crimson King." Closing the show with "21st Century Schizoid Man" was so fucking epic because it was the perfect, insane, mind-melting closing to an already epically mental and emotional evening.

Seeing King Crimson live was nothing short of a life changing experience for me. Their music is a beautiful, chaotic tapestry that overwhelmed my senses and changed the way I will think of music forever. Two songs in particular made an everlasting impression on me.

"Confusion will be my epitaph
As I crawl a cracked and broken path
If we make it, we can all sit back and laugh
But I fear, tomorrow, I'll be crying." – Epitaph

"Sundown dazzling day
Gold through my eyes
But my eyes turned within
Only see
Starless and bible black." – Starless

The combination of the imaginative lyrics and the hauntingly gorgeous music was nothing less than poetry in motion. These songs and all of the others that I heard that night rattled me to the core with a rollercoaster of emotions. I cried, laughed, and at times found myself slightly uncomfortable and somewhat disturbed by the bi-polar nature of the songs. It's a moment I wish I could relive over and over again, as it was one of the single greatest experiences of my life as a music lover.

I have gone back and tried to listen to some of Crimson's albums, and while I have this newfound love and appreciation for them, it's this current lineup that seems to be the one that ultimately captured me. Maybe this experience will affect how I hear some of the previous bands, maybe not. All I know is that it was this league of extraordinary gentlemen who found their way in and changed my life. By allowing myself to be open to the experience, I felt as if the barn doors to my soul were thrown open, and where there was once this void, King Crimson resides there happily forever for me to enjoy whenever I need to.

Rock N' Roll some of the nites and
a little bit on Sunday.
Me & my friends Jacob and Matt at the KISS Expo.
Atlanta, GA, 2018

Enlisted: The KISS Army

My first exposure to KISS was at the tender age of five when my parents were watching the made for TV movie *KISS Meets the Phantom of the Park*. If you haven't seen it, take a few puffs, find it on YouTube, and watch the members of KISS use their superpowers (Paul can shoot a laser from his star eye that allows him to control people's minds) to save…wait for it…an amusement park. This is some seriously trippy shit. Anyway, back to 1978. I was five, and according to my mom, the minute the music started in the movie, I ran into the kitchen, grabbed a broom, and started yelling, "Rock n' Roll! Rock n' Roll!" She turned to my dad and said, "Any ideas we had of Donald becoming a doctor or a lawyer are now gone!" Oh, Mom, if only you knew.

I don't remember the kitchen performance, but I do remember all of my KISS toys that followed it. I mean, KISS was pretty much the *Star Wars* of rock n' roll when it came to merchandising. Just about everything had the KISS logo plastered on it. Portable AM radios, fireman hats (for the song "Firehouse"), makeup kits, sleeping bags, and a Mego corporation line of KISS dolls complete with costumes and cardboard guitars. I was all-in. I had the Ace Frehley doll, KISS Colorforms, and even a KISS sleeping bag I would bring over to my grandma's house to sleep in. Hell, I slept in that damn thing so much that it fell apart in the washing machine.

So, if you walked into my childhood room, it looked like I was a huge KISS fan, but one thing was missing: I didn't *listen* to KISS. I had a Spirit of '77 poster on my wall, but I couldn't name you a single song. Then *Empire Strikes Back* came out, and like the fickle seven-year-old that I was, KISS became a thing of my past, and *Star Wars* took over my life for the next several years.

Fast forward to 1985. I was watching *Friday Night Videos* and saw the video for "Heaven's on Fire." I remember thinking, "Wow, they look old without their makeup on, but they still rock." That year for Christmas, I asked for two KISS albums: *Animalize* and *Double Platinum*. I dug the hell out of *Animalize,* but *Double Platinum* is what opened the doors for me (even then, I should have known that the best place to start with a band was a greatest hits collection). Next was *Destroyer*, then *Alive*, and then *Alive II*. After that, I think I bought every KISS record I could, regardless of quality.

I have to admit, as much as I loved KISS, their music never made an impact on me the way that Iron Maiden, Twisted Sister, and Dio did. While Maiden helped me not feel so alone in the world, KISS just put me in a good mood. KISS's misogynistic lyrics, even at a young age, were cringe-worthy to say the least. I remember my dad seeing the "Heavens on Fire" video and explaining to me that men

224

should never treat women like that. It was advice that wasn't taken lightly, but I still loved KISS in all of their stupid, crotch rock glory.

KISS made everything sound fun, and their live shows were legendary. I'm talking over the top spectacles with lights, stairs, ramps, and enough pyrotechnics to destroy New Jersey. Seeing KISS live is an amazing experience. Even though they are incredible businessmen who are able to merchandize the fuck out of the franchise (seriously, who needs a KISS Kasket? Wait a minute, that's actually a practical piece of merch for a diehard KISS fan), when they were on stage, it was all about making sure everyone there had a good time.

I saw them on for the first time on the *Crazy Nights* tour, and it blew my mind. Then I saw the *Hot in the Shade* tour and then the *Revenge* tour. From the post-apocalyptic New York City stage set up to the insanely awesome setlist, I thought that the *Revenge* tour was the best of the best up to that point. That is until it was announced that all four original members of KISS were reuniting after a successful *Unplugged* performance on MTV for the *Alive/Worldwide* tour.

That's right. Ace Frehley, Peter Criss, Paul Stanley, and Gene Simmons back in makeup, full costumes, embarking on a huge ass tour, and you bet your sweet ass that on October 2, 1996 in Atlanta, GA, I was losing my mind up in the nosebleed seats. I was there by myself, but I wasn't alone. What do I mean by that? Well, when you are part of the KISS Army, even if you're by yourself at a show, you're with your comrades; your battalion is right there with you to shout it out loud.

The KISS Army is truly something special. It's a fan base unlike any other. They're sort of like Deadheads in that their allegiance to the band is undying, but these folks don't fuck around. I mean, does the word "army" equate with anything half-hearted? These folks proudly sport tattoos of their favorite KISS members, album covers, and even lyrics. Some folks go as far as to name their children after members of the band, although I have yet to meet anyone named Ace.

Every year, in multiple cities across the country (probably the world), KISS fans gather for KISS Expos, which are one or two days of organized dorking out. People get decked out in their costumes and face paint (the quality varies), and fans scour the rows of vendor tables to try to find coveted pieces of KISS memorabilia that they just had to have.

I've always wanted to attend one of these Expos, and I got my chance in January of 2018. Not only was I getting to go with a VIP pass (damn, my life is good), this was also going to mark the first public appearance of estranged KISS guitarist Vinnie Vincent in over twenty years. There was an air of excitement in the place. However, the venue itself—the unassuming fourth floor of a generic Marriott hotel in suburban Atlanta—left a lot to be desired. There wasn't even any quality signage letting you know that this awesome event was happening.

But it was the place to find some pretty cool shit. There were trading cards, overpriced KISS Mego dolls, and some cool vinyl pieces. Some vendors were also selling just the inserts from various KISS albums, which I thought was brilliant. I managed to score the much sought-after German pressing of *KISS Killers* (with the block S's) and even picked up a KISS Love Gun pop gun insert that I have wanted to replace for over thirty years.

After doing some shopping, I checked out some of the special guest appearances. The first one I ran into was guitarist Bob Kulick. On my blog, I didn't give Bob's debut solo album (or the artwork) the most glowing review. Luckily, he had no clue who I was and had no problem posing for a photo with me. I talked with him for about five minutes, and he was seriously the sweetest, kindest person you could imagine with none of the egos I thought he would have. He was a super nice dude, and it was a real honor to meet him.

I continued to stroll the room when all of a sudden, I heard a familiar voice complaining and bitching and saying shit like, "What am I supposed to be doing?" "Where do I go? This thing is so unorganized." Blah blah blah. I turned around, and sure enough, it's Eddie Trunk. Eddie Trunk is a DJ in New York who has his own show called *The Eddie Trunk Show*. He also hosted *That Metal Show* on VH1 for a while until it was finally cancelled. I have never liked Trunk because of his pompous, smug, know it all attitude. I have been pretty vocal about my feelings on my blog and social media and seeing him at this event just solidified my disliking of him.

Trunk looked right at me, and I doubted that he had heard of my blog or knew how much shit talking I had done about him. I asked him for a photo, and he said in a grumpy voice, "Make it quick." Oh man, this was my moment. So I posed with ol' shithead for a selfie, and then I take a second one flying a middle finger over his head. I waited for years to troll him in person, and now I can die a happy blogger. He was every bit the pompous, arrogant ass I imagined he'd be. I really wouldn't have minded him proving me wrong, but dude just confirmed to me that he's a Grade A windbag tool.

My favorite part of the whole experience was getting to meet fans from all over the world. I met fans from Germany, Sweden, Australia, and Canada and chatted with great folks from Florida who were wearing homemade KISS costumes that looked fantastic. Sharing our favorite KISS-related stories, I truly felt like I was with my tribe. It was a reminder of what a magical band KISS is. To have a fan base this rabid that are just as excited to hang out with other fans as they are to meet the band members themselves says a lot. I mean, this is the KISS Army after all. We are a unified family bonded together by this awe-inspiring band with silly lyrics and over the top image.

I officially joined the KISS Army in 1985. Although I have since lost my patch and all of my fan club memorabilia, once a member of the KISS Army, always a member. KISS is a very special band that found a way to bring together the outcasts, the freaks, the loners, and the geeks, and assemble an army that would go into battle anytime KISS came to town to defend the right to rock n' roll all nite, and party every day.

When Dreams and Reality Unite

The idea of meeting a rock star was unfathomable when I was a kid. As I got older, meeting my favorite rock stars became somewhat of a mission. Not necessarily because I wanted to go all Beatles fangirl on them but because I sincerely wanted to have the opportunity to thank them for making the music that meant so much to me. Going to arena shows made it damn near impossible to meet Iron Maiden, KISS, Alice Cooper, etc. So many people, security, and barricades kept all of us creeps away from these poor people who worked so hard to entertain us.

As I got older and started going to club shows, I found that it was easier to meet bands. The tour bus was generally parked right outside the venue, and if you hung out long enough, you could meet a band member or two. Whether or not they were going to be cool was a whole different story. I remember waiting in the rain to meet the Ramones for an hour after a show once. Johnny Ramone came out first and blew right past us and got into the van. I couldn't believe he was just feet away from me and that I wasn't going to meet him. CJ Ramone took the time to shake some hands and sign a few things, but I was still bummed that Johnny didn't seem interested in meeting his fans. But then he stepped out of the van and said, "Might as well," and he ended up being so nice. I was so proud of my still sealed vintage copy of *Road to Ruin*, and he said, "Oh, this is cool." and then tore the shrink wrap off to sign it. A part of me died, but a part of me was ecstatic that I had a Johnny Ramone signed album. Unfortunately, I sold it many years ago when I was having some hard times, but you know, the memory of that exchange will never go away.

There were many other cool ones. Faster Pussycat played here in Atlanta once, and we waited and waited and waited for them to exit the venue. Their opening act, Slik Toxik, came out and they were so down to earth and personable. They took the time to talk to my friends and me, signed our cigarette packs and ticket stubs, and just shot the shit with us. The singer Nick Walsh and guitarist Kevin Gale had both bummed cigarettes off of me. Later that evening, Kevin Gale came over to me with a fresh pack of Marlboro Reds and said, "Thanks for the smoke when I couldn't find mine." They talked to us and laughed, and they were so fucking cool.

The guys in Faster Pussycat, on the other hand, were complete dicks and had zero time to talk to us except for their drummer, Brett Bradshaw. He was nice and gave us all drumsticks and talked a bit. We thought the other dudes were just assholes, but as a musician myself, I know how emotionally and physically exhausting a live show can be. Maybe that was it. Maybe they *were* dicks. Who knows?

When Saigon Kick was at their peak with their album *The Lizard*, they came to Atlanta and played a packed house at the Masquerade. After the show, we waited by their tour bus, and lead singer Matt Kramer was the only one to talk to us. I told him how much he reminded me of a modern Jim Morrison, and we talked at length about The Doors. He was so cordial with us, and when guitarist Jason Bieler came out, we tried to talk to him, but he just walked up to me, put a pick in my hand, boarded the bus, and that was it. Many years later in 2019, I shared this moment with Jason via Facebook and we had a good laugh about it. He told me about how hard it was to be on the road and that sometimes he was in a funk over something. Maybe it was a bad show for him or maybe he wasn't feeling well. It was cool to bond with him over this experience and we have since spoken many times and become buddies. Life is weird sometimes.

Babylon A.D. was one of the coolest bands I met from that era. They were experiencing some success at the time but seemed to be completely unaffected by it. I had the pleasure of meeting them three different times, and every time, they remembered me and my buddies and hooked us up with picks, drumsticks, and even tour shirts. They were genuinely kind and very appreciative of our support. It was interactions like these that would eventually shape how I would approach meeting rock stars as a writer.

Since starting my blog in 2009, I can't even begin to tell you how many of my favorite musicians I have met. Now don't get me wrong; I'm not saying this to brag. Ok, I *am* saying this to brag. Why the fuck not? I'm super proud of the artists I've had the opportunity to meet. In some instances, meeting artists as a writer is different than meeting them as a fan, but in most situations, surprisingly, the musicians I've met are more human and more real than I thought they would ever be.

Interviewing and meeting some of my all-time favorites has been an interesting experience. I would say that easily ninety percent are genuinely kind, sweet, humble folks who truly enjoy meeting their fans. To this day, at an Exodus show, you can find Steve "Zetro" Souza hanging out by the busses taking photos, signing autographs, and talking to fans just like he's one of them. He was every bit as humble and kind with those people as he was with me during an interview.

It has been a dream come true to become friends with musicians I have admired for years such as Jeff Keith of Tesla, Bobby Caldwell of Captain Beyond, and Jordan Rudess of Dream Theater. I've also had the pleasure of meeting some great up-and-comers including Kyng, Holy Grail, Savage Master, Jess and the Ancient Ones, Brave, and Electric Citizen. I've become very close friends with various members. To able to strike up a friendship with them and see how well they interact with their fans is a testament to their realness.

I've said this a lot, but I am a very lucky human being. I'm living an amazing life, doing things that I and many others only ever dreamed of as a kid. I've hung out on tour busses, interviewed bands, shared meals with artists whose posters adorned my bedroom walls as a kid, and in some cases, I've become legitimate friends where we talk on the phone and text. It's without a doubt a dream come true and something I don't take for granted. The fact that I have developed a loyal, dedicated readership on The Great Southern Brainfart who share an interest in following me on this exciting journey is something I never thought would happen.

In September of 1992, after a Motorhead show, I was waiting for hours for legendary bassist/front man Lemmy Kilmister to emerge from the backstage door. I had nothing for him to sign, no camera for pictures, nothing. All I wanted was to tell this guy how much his music meant to me. Lemmy came down the backstage stairs outside the venue with two lovely ladies in tow. He saw me standing there, and I said, "Hey Lemmy, thanks for the music." Lemmy stopped and replied, "Hey, man, are you cool?" "Not at all," I said. Lemmy just smiled and said, "You will be, mate. Cheers." and walked away.

I don't know that I would consider myself cool, but I will say that Lemmy's words rang true in a certain sense. That fat, loser, dork kid who dreamed big and loved even bigger turned out just fine. I wish Lemmy was here to read this, but wherever he is, I'd like to think that he's drinking a Jack and Coke and saying, "Fuck yeah, mate. You did it."

Acknowledgements

Thank you to....

my wife and best friend Lizzi. From the very beginning, you loved me for being a dreamer. You encouraged me, supported me, and never allowed me to give up anything without a fight. You put in hours with me to make this book the best that it could be. I couldn't have done any of this without you. I love you more than anything.

my mother who took me to heavy metal concerts and who had to listen to me learn how to the electric guitar. You were so patient with me and never complained. I love you so much.

my in-laws Dick and Marge for being the best "other" parents anyone could ask for. Your love and encouragement mean so much to me and I love you both.

my brother, Dwayne. You were a pain in my ass for so many years, but the memories of you and me blasting music, collecting magazines, and hanging posters are ones I'll never forget.

James Hines. I can always count on you to give it to me straight even when I don't want to hear it. Thanks for all the great years of friendship and here's to many more.

Bert Wray. Your brotherhood, laughs, and amazing conversations about writing always inspire me. I am proud to call you brother.

Katherine Turman. You are a mentor, my editor, and most importantly, my friend. You continue to inspire me with your passion and love for all things writing.

Jon Freeman. Thanks for all the years of friendship and for giving me shit for not liking half the music you send me. Thank you for also turning me on to some of the best music I would have never heard.

Lilly Ryden, Amy Sciarretto, and Loana Valencia. You all answered my emails back when nobody would. Thanks for believing in me, rooting me on, and virtually high-fiving me.

My band mates Alison Shockely and Luis Nieves. You both inspire me and encourage me to share my life through words and song. Thanks for being in my life.

Jacob Moulder for not just listening to my rock n' roll stories but for sharing yours with me as well. Burgers, beers, and many more laughs are in our future.

Michelle Schrotz. You are the perfect example of how I have made some amazing friends doing my blog. Thanks for being a friend.

Last but definitely not least, thank you to all of my dedicated The Great Southern Brainfart readers. From the very beginning in 2009, you have inspired me, antagonized me, loved me, and hated me. It's because of each one of you that I continue to do this with all the love and passion that I can give it. Thank you all.

In this book, I shared some of the difficult experiences that I faced growing up. I am thankful that I made it through (thanks Dee, Ronnie, Alice, and others).

Bullying and depression can be experienced by people of all ages. If you need someone to talk to, there are people who can help.

National Suicide Prevention Lifeline: 1-800-273-TALK
National Alliance on Mental Illness: 1-800-950-NAMI
Substance Abuse Helpline: 1-800-662-HELP

Made in the USA
Columbia, SC
01 March 2020